M000304454

POSITIVE
CASH
FLOW

POWERFUL TOOLS AND TECHNIQUES
TO COLLECT YOUR RECEIVABLES,
MANAGE YOUR PAYABLES, AND FUEL
YOUR GROWTH

WITHDRAWN

By

Robert A. Cooke

SCHAUMBURG TOWNSHIP DISTRICT LIBRARY
130 SOUTH ROSELLE ROAD
SCHAUMBURG, ILLINOIS 60193

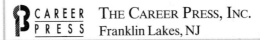

CAREER PRESS   THE CAREER PRESS, INC.
Franklin Lakes, NJ

3 1257 01475 6745

Copyright © 2003 by Robert A. Cooke

All rights reserved under the Pan-American and International Copyright Conventions. This book may not be reproduced, in whole or in part, in any form or by any means electronic or mechanical, including photocopying, recording, or by any information storage and retrieval system now known or hereafter invented, without written permission from the publisher, The Career Press.

POSITIVE CASH FLOW
EDITED BY CLAYTON W. LEADBETTER
TYPESET BY EILEEN DOW MUNSON
Cover design by The Visual Group
Printed in the U.S.A. by Book-mart Press

To order this title, please call toll-free 1-800-CAREER-1 (NJ and Canada: 201-848-0310) to order using VISA or MasterCard, or for further information on books from Career Press.

CAREER
PRESS

The Career Press, Inc., 3 Tice Road, PO Box 687,
Franklin Lakes, NJ 07417
www.careerpress.com

Library of Congress Cataloging-in-Publication Data

Cooke, Robert A., 1931-
   Positive cash flow : powerful tools and techniques to collect your receivables, manage
   your payables, and fuel your growth / by Robert A. Cooke.
      p. cm.
   Includes index.
   ISBN 1-56414-677-4 (paper)
      1. Cash management. 2. Cash flow. 3. Accounts receivable—Management.
      4. Accounts payable—Management. I. Title.

   HG4028.C45C578 2003
   658.15'244—dc21

                                                      2003043454

To my wife,
Carolyn,
who inspires me to apply seat to chair
and fingers to keyboard,
supplies support with suggestions
for words and phrases
that "keep it simple,"
and also corrects my flawed concept of punctuation.

Acknowledgments

This book would not have been possible without the efforts and assistance of many people, especially my publisher, Ron Fry, and the crew at Career Press, including Mike Lewis, Clayton Leadbetter, Eileen Munson, Gina Cheselka, and Stacey A. Farkas.

And a special thank-you goes to Gene Brissie, my agent, who not only keeps me busy but frequently supplies encouragement and advice.

Contents

CHAPTER 1

Where to Find the Cash

"Could you use extra cash?" That may be the most over-used and meaningless phrase in advertising. The obvious answer, of course, is: Who couldn't? Even those businesses with large cash balances could use more still for new ventures, bigger dividends, higher salaries, and more stock options for the CEO. We all wish for a source that would just dump extra cash into our coffers, with no strings attached, and allow us to use that cash as we see fit, even if it's only for our own enjoyment. Unfortunately those sources, outside of the lottery, do not exist.

So the money comes with strings. Investors want collateral, interest, dividends, and, sometimes, to participate in the management of your business. Customers want products and services, and sometimes they want to use *your* money before they send it to you many months later.

Here are the most common sources of funds:

Borrow the Funds

There are two classes of investors for most businesses: those who loan money to the business and those who make an equity investment in the business. That is, rather than loaning money to the business, equity investors actually buy a piece of the business in hopes that someday it will be worth many big bucks. Let's first look at the sources of borrowing:

Banks

Need money? The first place most of us think of is our local bank. Here it is, after all, in the business of loaning money, so why wouldn't you try there first? And indeed, that's not a bad idea. You've probably heard the old saying "banks only loan money to people who don't need it." To some extent that's true, but remember that banks will loan money to people who do need it, *if* the bank is pretty certain to be repaid. How does a bank make sure that it will get its money back? It may loan you money if it can:

+ Grab some of your property if you fail to send the money back when it's due. In other words, the bank wants collateral.

+ Make sure that someone else is on the hook to pay the bank if you don't. In other words, the bank wants a guarantor.

+ Convince itself that your business will be so successful that there is no way you would not have enough cash with which to repay the loan.

Put up Collateral for the Bank

The most common example of borrowing with collateral is the process in which you give the bank a mortgage on your house, and the bank loans you money—probably. If you are in business or about to go into business, arranging a line of credit, secured by the equity on your house, should be one of your first tasks. The interest rate should be lower than for any other form of business financing, and you don't pay any interest until you draw funds from the line of credit. If you're starting a business, get this financing approved before you quit your day job! Even if you have lots of equity in your house, it's tougher to borrow money when your only source of income is from your new business.

Don't overlook other types of collateral that may appeal to the bank. If you plan on using your car, boat, or airplane for collateral, this is definitely an area where you should arrange that financing before quitting your current job. Obviously, those assets lose their value over time, so banks don't value them as highly as real estate, and they'll generally charge a higher rate of interest for loans secured in this way.

If you have any stocks and bonds from highly rated, publicly held companies, they can be very acceptable collateral for a bank That raises the question of why not just sell securities to generate the cash? Think income tax. If you look at our income tax structure, you'll realize the sale of those securities will probably mean that you owe the IRS money, and you'll have only part of the sale proceeds for your business. If you use the securities as collateral, all of the proceeds of the bank loan are yours to use in your business. Be aware, though, that you do continue with the market risk. That is, if the securities decrease substantially in value, the bank may insist that you put up more collateral. If you fail to do that, the bank may sell your securities, thereby incurring a tax bill for you.

Guarantees by Other People or Businesses

The second enticement that may cause the bank to provide funds to you is a personal guarantee. Obviously, he or she who guarantees this loan for you needs to have substantial net worth, and some of that net worth needs to be easily converted into cash. So, if your Uncle Harry's wealth is made up of stocks, bonds, certificates of deposit, and other liquid investments that can be sold easily and quickly, he may be attractive as a guarantor. However, if his wealth is in the office building, the farm, his waterfront home, and an oriental rug collection, he wouldn't be so attractive as a guarantor, for it takes time and much expense to sell those types of assets. If your business went belly-up and the bank had to call on Uncle Harry to pay off the loan, it could take months or years for him to convert a piece of property or a rug into cash with which he could pay the bank.

Of course, Uncle Harry could directly loan the money to your business, but maybe he wants to keep his money working in Wal-Mart (he owns much Wal-Mart stock) rather than in your business. The guarantee route enables him to keep his investment and help you at the same time.

Don't be surprised if your banker won't accept a guarantee. Some banks have been burned by poorly worded guarantees that were unenforceable.

Your solution? Try another bank.

Government
(Small Business Administration)

If your Uncle Harry won't come through with big bucks for you, there's another choice—and that's your Uncle Sam, in the form of the Small Business Administration (SBA). Generally, if the entrepreneur fills out all the paperwork and passes some basic screening, the SBA will guarantee a portion of the loan that a commercial bank makes to a business.

Sally started the Slow Software Company by borrowing $500,000 from the local bank. The bank loaned her the money because she presented a business plan that made it appear that the business would be successful, and, most importantly, the SBA guaranteed 75 percent of the loan.

Sally worked hard, but the company was slow to bring new products to market, and competitors grabbed most of her customers. After three years, she was unable to even pay interest on the loan and had to declare her company bankrupt. As she still owed a balance of $400,000, the bank was not happy. However, it was not as unhappy as it could have been, for the bank did not lose the $400,000, but only 25 percent of that amount. The government, through the SBA, swallowed the $300,000 representing the rest of the loss.

Incidentally, if you have a business that can be located in an economically disadvantaged area (such as "inner city") and hire the residents of that area, there is an SBA program to provide more support (additional financing) for your business. Also, you then may be eligible for tax breaks available to companies that so locate.

How do you contact the SBA? Check Appendix E for more information about SBA loans.

Note that in discussing guarantees, we have been using the term in the sense that one person guarantees the debts of another person. The word *guarantee* is also often used in a situation in which a business is incorporated, and the owners (stockholders) guarantee the debts of the business. To further explain, let's change Sally's situation slightly:

Instead of operating as a sole proprietor, in which case Sally would be known as "Sally Smith, doing business as the Slow Software Company," she decided to operate her business as a corporation. It was called "The Slow Software Company, Incorporated." If she borrowed from the bank as a sole proprietor, she would automatically be liable for the debts of the business personally, so she would need to provide the bank with only a guarantee from the SBA. If she operated as a corporation, the bank would demand that she personally guarantee the debts of the corporation as well as provide a guarantee from the SBA. Additionally, she would have to provide a personal guarantee to the SBA.

Many entrepreneurs make the mistake of thinking that, if they form a corporation and then cause the corporation to borrow funds with which to start a business, they will not be responsible for repaying the loan personally. That is, they believe that doing business within a corporate shell will protect them from lawsuits, judgments, liens, and other nasty things that can occur in our economic lives. Theoretically, they are right. But practically, that's not the real world. Those who loan money (bankers, usually) will say, "Tough. If you want the money, you have to sign the personal guarantee." So sign it, buy good liability insurance, and hope for the best.

A Strong Business Plan

The third process that may entice a bank to cough up funds for your business is that of convincing the bank's loan officer that your business can't help but make mucho bucks, and of being so convincing that the bank will make a loan to you and your business without collateral or a guarantee from a wealthy friend or relative. How do you do that? The process consists of putting together an impressive, irrefutable business plan, and that's not easy. Writing a business plan is a subject that can fill an entire book, which is why it's only mentioned here. However, see Appendix F for some sources of help in creating a business plan and some do's and don'ts derived from my own experience. Suffice it to say that it is virtually impossible to attract bank financing based only on the business plan if the business is new. As the business matures and proves its profitability, attracting unsecured bank financing based on only the merits of the business becomes a possibility. But even for a seasoned business, the well-written and fully documented business plan usually is a necessity.

Friends and Relatives

Maybe you're one of the lucky ones who has a rich relative or friend, and by "rich," I mean someone who is comfortably well-off but not a billionaire who would not miss a few hundred thousand dollars. Tread carefully in this area, for one of the surest methods of losing a friend or alienating a relative is to borrow money from them and not pay it back, not because you don't want to pay it back, but because you can't. In other words, if your business goes bust (and we all hope it doesn't) you'll have trouble buying groceries, let alone paying back a loan of a few hundred thousand dollars.

Ralph wanted to start the No-Hole Doughnut Company, but he was unsuccessful in finding a bank to loan him start-up capital, regardless of whether or not the SBA would guarantee the loan. However, he had previously borrowed money from his Aunt Alice, who is moderately wealthy. Indeed, Aunt Alice was impressed by the responsible way in which Ralph had always quickly repaid the few hundred dollars that he had borrowed from her from time to time. Based on that good experience, she loaned her favorite nephew $300,000 with which he could start a small doughnut shop. Unfortunately, people seem to prefer old-fashioned doughnuts with the hole in the middle, so customers at Ralph's doughnut shop were scarce. The bottom line was that Ralph had to close the shop and return to his previous job at a fast food restaurant. How was Ralph going to repay his aunt? He couldn't. This meant that Aunt Alice had to reconsider her early retirement plans and continue to work until she was well past retirement age. Was Ralph still her favorite nephew? I doubt it.

Whether you are a new or existing business, it's important that you document the borrowing of the funds by a formal note, which specifies the repayment schedule, the interest rate, and any other terms to which you have verbally agreed. In other words, try to keep the business relationship separate from the family relationship or friendship.

As for other terms that may be agreed upon, you may find that, in order to entice someone to loan funds to your business, you may have to agree that if you cannot meet the terms of the note, the lender will become a part-owner of the business and will participate in management decisions. Making such an agreement may later prove to be wise or unwise, but it may be the only means by which you can attract someone to loan funds to your business.

Other Places to Borrow Money

Sometimes the difference between success and failure is the ability to be creative. If you're starting a business, include financing in your discussions with others who have succeeded in your chosen business. (This is the tried-and-true advice that you should visit people in the same business who are outside of your marketing area. In other words, if you are going to start a pet supply store, visit others in that business who are more than 50 miles away from you and out of your market area. People seem to like to talk about their successes, but not with direct competitors.)

The same advice (to visit others outside of your area) holds for those who are already in business. Add the trade association for your business to your list of resources. It may be able to offer suggestions for financing sources.

Suppliers

Don't overlook suppliers as a source of funds. If you buy supplies or raw materials from an industry that is competitive, you may well find that suppliers will loan you money in order to gain your business. They may not be eager to scratch out a check and hand it to you, but they may provide an initial order with easy payment terms. This amounts to the same thing as a bank loan, if you were to use the proceeds to buy those supplies.

> When Ralph started his doughnut shop, the Slippery Cooking Oil Company really wanted his business, so it delivered $1,000 worth of oil to Ralph's shop. The invoice specified that the total invoice could be paid in increments of $100 per month for a period of 10 months. Inasmuch as the invoice called for just the 10 payments of $100, it was a better deal than borrowing from the bank, as the deal from the Slippery Cooking Oil Company amounted to a zero-interest loan.

It may be possible to arrange longer-term financing with suppliers, but be careful what you sign, as such arrangements may amount to the lender getting most of the profits from your business. Some years ago, this situation existed in the bar business, and it may still exist some places:

> Bernie wanted to open the Guzzle-Down Tavern, but his total resources amounted to $287.52. He needed

$10,000 with which to do some needed repairs to the building, pay the first month's rent, and pay for an initial stock of beer and pickled pig's feet. As you might expect, banks are not anxious to finance start-up taverns. His wealthy Aunt Susan was a teetotaler, so Bernie had to look for financing any place he could find it. Those were the days when neighborhood bars kept the television volume low so that customers could carry on a conversation and listen to music from the coin-operated jukebox. That's where Bernie found money.

The Money Bags Music Company that supplied the machines and records for the music had a program to help new entrepreneurs. It would loan Bernie $10,000 at 40 percent interest per year. (That state's usury laws did not cover business loans.) Bernie had to agree that Money Bags would be the only provider of music in the tavern, and it would collect the money from the music machine. Bernie would be credited with a percentage of those collections, but Money Bags would keep its share of the cash and apply it towards payment of the principal and interest of the loan. Needless to say, it took a lot of quarters to make the loan payments, so Bernie never saw any extra cash from the collections. He constantly had to add to the collections in order to pay just the interest on the loan.

> Moral: Read all agreements carefully before signing. Compute the resulting cash flow and back away from any deal that won't be profitable. (The computations are covered in Chapter 4.)

Customers

Yes, customers can be a source of financing. If you're in a custom job business, such as a print shop or custom construction, you should be requiring substantial deposits on work before it is undertaken. Creating custom work that is suitable only for one customer, without any deposit, is sheer folly even if the customer has repeatedly done business with you several times in the past.

If you have hard-to-find expertise, and a customer is in great need of your skills and knowledge, you may be able to extract a long-term financing arrangement from the customer. This is particularly true if the customer is a large, well-financed company.

Credit Cards and Charge Accounts

Normally, credit cards and charge accounts should be used as a convenience. That is, they should be paid off monthly, so that no high-rate interest is charged and you have an ample line of credit for future business purchases. But there may well come a day when a crisis will arise and these cards will be the only immediate source of cash that can keep your business alive. Use them if you must, but at the same time make arrangements for other financing at a smaller interest charge and better repayment terms. (You should make these other arrangements even if there is no other reason than to open up the line of credit represented by credit cards and charge accounts.)

Some people have financed business ventures strictly from maxing out several credit cards. When that process proves to be the basis for a successful business, it's news that makes the business magazines. What doesn't get published are the many more businesses that try to exist on credit card financing and end up in bankruptcy court.

Summary of Borrowing

Not even Bill Gates or a Saudi prince has unlimited funds. Your funds are, no doubt, considerably more limited than theirs, so borrowing becomes a fact of your business life. The key is planning, and there's a great deal about that in Chapter 4. For now, keep in mind that you need to be positive that there will be enough cash flow to meet your scheduled payments.

Some final thoughts about borrowing are in the "Do" and "Don't" lists that follow:

Do

☑ Arrange for loans well before you may need the funds.

☑ Negotiate a line of credit so you won't be paying interest on funds that you don't yet need.

☑ Try for a loan on which you pay only interest for several months before you have to pay something on the principal of the loan.

☑ Put promissory notes and other agreements with lenders (even your mother) in writing.

☑ Plan to use your own money last. Use other people's money first. That way, when you need those last few dollars to tide your business through a dry spell, that decision to use those funds is entirely up to you.

Don't

☒ Pay exorbitant interest rates. If that is the only way you can obtain start-up or expansion funds, rethink your business strategy.

☒ Agree to quick repayment of the loan or a balloon payment.

☒ Arrange a short-term loan (a bridge loan) in anticipation of being able to repay the lender by the proceeds from long-term financing, unless you already have a solid commitment for the long-term loan.

Equity Investors

It would be great if you could decide to open a pizza restaurant and immediately walk into Merrill Lynch and sign up for an initial public stock offering of several million dollars. Then you could immediately open 25 pizza restaurants. Unfortunately, such a scenario happens only in daydreams. Yes, there was a time, in the late 1990s, when you could almost do that. It wouldn't happen with new pizza restaurant companies, but if you had a novel computer or software product, it might have happened. But those days are gone, with the end of most of the e-something start-ups in the bursting of the dotcom bubble.

Although your proposed or existing business may be too small for a public stock offering, that doesn't mean you can't find equity investors—that is, people who would like a part of the ownership in your business if they are to provide funds for its operation.

Venture Capitalists

Venture capitalists come in various shapes and forms. Some specialize in certain industries, some specialize in only those businesses that have existed for several years, and some will actually be interested in brand-new businesses. However, if you're starting a brand-new business and do not have significant management experience in that line of business, you can virtually forget about venture capitalists. Remember that venture capital firms receive hundreds of proposals each week. Only about 2 or 3 percent of those proposals make it through the first glance and into the "maybe" pile.

Before you submit a proposal to any venture capitalist, do your homework. At the very least, your proposal should include a business plan that includes projected financial statements and, most importantly, projected cash flow. (See Chapter 4 for details on the cash flow projection.) Back up every statement you make in the proposal with fact. For instance, when you state a projected sales figure, include the basis for that figure. It could be demographics of a retail area, traffic counts at competitors' locations, focus groups' opinions, and so on.

Relatives, Friends, and Others

The same people who we discussed as possible sources of loans could also be equity investors. Indeed, some of them may prefer to be equity investors because, as venture capitalists do, they stand to make a far higher return on their funds than they would by loaning the money to you at a nominal interest rate. In other words, Ralph and Aunt Alice might have been better off if she had taken an equity position (part-ownership) in Ralph's doughnut shop for these reasons:

✦ The No-Hole Doughnut Shop would not have had to make interest payments to Aunt Alice during the start-up, which might have made enough difference in the shop's cash flow to prevent having to close the store before it could become profitable.

✦ Although Aunt Alice would have had to wait until the business was profitable for a return on her investment, she would have been compensated for her wait by a higher return on her investment in the future.

✦ Aunt Alice, as a part-owner, might have felt more incentive to offer suggestions and advice to Ralph. (Nobody can operate successfully in a vacuum.)

Structuring the Equity Investment (Taking in a Partner)

If, in order to inject more cash into your new or existing business, you take in a partner, do take care. Many partnerships fail, not so much because of lack of cash flow, but lack of a formal agreement between the partners. The partners spend too much time arguing between themselves and not enough time tending to business, and that results in a lack of cash flow. Often there is little agreement as to who will invest how much in the partnership, who will invest additional funds if needed, and what will be the duties and management responsibilities of each partner. This happens very often because a partnership is formed by two friends deciding to go into business together but making few, if any, other decisions. Some of these other decisions would include:

✦ How are major management disagreements to be resolved (use of a third party advisor, flip of a coin, etc.)?

✦ What are the daily responsibilities of each partner (sales, production, hiring, etc.)?

✦ How much time will each partner devote to the partnership's business?

✦ What will be the initial investment of each partner, and how much additional investment will be required of each partner?

✦ What else is important in the business?

Discuss these terms with your prospective partner. If you can't agree on terms at this point, the chance of success if you become partners is highly unlikely.

Once you have an outline of your agreements, have a business-oriented attorney wrap them up in a document that complies with state laws and then have a CPA review it for workability in the financial area and the resulting tax effects.

Instead of a partnership arrangement with which to bring in equity capital, consider a corporation. The corporate form makes it easier to specify who owns how much of the business (as determined by the stock owned). You can also get fairly fancy with a corporation, by having some stock voting (control) and some stock nonvoting. This sometimes can be attractive to an investor who does not want to get actively involved in the business operations. You can also do such things as issue preferred stock, which allows an investor to receive specified dividends before other stockholders can take money out of business. Even fancier than that is a concept of convertible preferred stock—stock that does not have voting rights but is guaranteed dividends before those who hold common stock receive any dividends. But in the event that profits decline below a certain level or cash and liquid assets decline below a certain level, the preferred stock becomes common stock with voting rights. If the investor then owns more than 50 percent of the stock, this can be attractive to him or her. If you mismanage the business to the extent that it does not become profitable, the investor can take over the management of the enterprise and try to salvage it.

There are many other considerations in selecting the form for the business and drawing agreements between partners and stockholders. Whole books have been written on this subject (some by this author), which should be read by any entrepreneur—particularly one who is going to need more capital than he or she has in the bank.

Summary of Equity Investors

Do

☑ Create a comprehensive business plan with plenty of supporting documentation. (This is necessary for both start-up and existing businesses.)

☑ Try venture capitalists, but know that the odds are slim.

☑ Keep it on a business footing, if you raise an investment in your business from friends, relatives, and associates, by having your agreement in comprehensive writing that is reviewed by professionals.

☑ Be careful how you structure the form of your business (partnership, limited liability company, or corporation). Obtain professional help on the tax (serious cash outflow) consequences.

Don't

☒ Pay exorbitant interest rates for borrowed funds.

☒ Give the store away to attract an equity investor, as in agreements that make it easy for him or her to take over your business.

Timely Collection of Accounts Receivable From Customers

This is an area in which poor management can directly create the demise of a business. Consider the following case of what letting a large customer charge its purchases did to profit:

> Ralph's No-Hole Doughnut Shop was five blocks from the Amalgamated Consolidated Corporation (ACC). When he opened his shop, several people from that company were his first customers, paying cash for doughnuts that they purchased for themselves and several coworkers. Most of the staff at ACC seemed to be more productive after partaking of Ralph's doughnuts, so the CEO of ACC authorized the corporate purchase of doughnuts from Ralph. However, the CEO did not want his financial people to have the hassle paying for the doughnuts with cash, so the CEO asked Ralph to extend credit to the ACC account for the daily doughnut purchases. Ralph accepted the deal and enjoyed the resulting significant increase in business. Table 1-1 shows his profit picture, for each doughnut.

Normal Profit on Sale of One Doughnut

Sale price of one doughnut		$ 1.00
Cost of doughnut		
Raw material	$ 0.35	
Labor to make doughnut	0.26	
Labor to package and deliver donut	0.25	
Overhead: rent, electricity, insurance, etc.	0.12	
Total cost of one doughnut		0.98
Net profit on each doughnut		$ 0.02

Table 1-1

However, Ralph didn't bank on the fact that ACC had a large accounts payable section, where employees were to pay bills from suppliers. This process involved a large bureaucracy that meant an invoice from the No-Hole Doughnut Shop had to go through several levels of approval before it could be paid. On average, this process took about four months. While Ralph waited for the payments from ACC to arrive, he had to borrow money at 12 percent annual interest. Including that cost in his profit-per-doughnut picture made it look like Table 1-2:

Profit on One Doughnut if Credit Extended

Sale price of one doughnut		$ 1.00
Cost of doughnut		
Raw material	$ 0.35	
Labor to make doughnut	0.26	
Labor to package and deliver donut	0.25	
Overhead: rent, electricity, insurance, etc.	0.12	
Interest on account receivable for one doughnut, two months	0.03	
Total cost of one doughnut		1.01
Net profit on each doughnut		$ (0.01)

Table 1-2

Instead of a net profit of two cents on each doughnut, Ralph suffered a loss of one cent on each doughnut purchased by ACC.

Admittedly, this deal may still make sense, for the sales to ACC do pay some overhead expense that otherwise would have to be paid by other customers. But, you should be aware of what extending credit to even major customers can do to your profitability.

(Please note that these figures may not be repre-
sentative of the doughnut industry. They were selected
in order to illustrate a principle.)

Your Credit Department
(You, if Your Business Is Small)

In addition to the interest expense, there are other costs
related to extension of credit by an entrepreneur. Among these
are the following:

✦ You, or an employee, must spend time checking
  out credit references and other background information before credit is extended.

✦ In order to check background information, you
  will incur the expense of one or more credit checking agencies, such as Dun & Bradstreet, Equifax,
  and so forth.

✦ Inevitably, there will be some people who will not
  pay on time, and some who would like to never
  pay. In such cases, you or an employee must spend
  time on the phone with slow-paying customers and
  collection attorneys, and possibly some time in
  court pursuing a collection.

✦ You will need an accounting system that makes the
  management of accounts receivable a relatively
  simple task.

✦ As a business owner, your time may be better spent
  in developing marketing strategies and making
  sales. Fortunately, there are some alternatives.

Credit and Debit Cards

These days, almost everyone who has ever paid a bill rates a credit card. There are some credit card issuers (banks, etc.) that specialize in issuing credit cards to high-risk individuals and some high-risk businesses. If you sell to low- and middle-income individuals and small businesses, you may be well advised to let the people who specialize in that sort of market take the risk for you. Of course, accepting credit cards entails some charges to you, the seller. If you have a high profit margin in your product, setting up to accept credit cards should be a no-brainer. If your profit margin is low, you are likely to be tempted to extend credit from your own pocket. Think carefully before following this route. Estimate the costs of handling credit, including the value of your own time, by doing a calculation similar to the process shown in Table 1-2. If you make these calculations honestly, you will probably find it is cheaper to use a credit card processing service. What you should do, though, is carefully shop for the best deal and the lowest rates for the credit card processing.

From a merchant's standpoint, debit cards operate almost like credit cards. The major difference, of course, is that rather than being a credit transaction, the money is taken directly out of the purchaser's bank account. When you shop for a merchant processing service, be sure that debit card processing is included, for without it, you inevitably will lose a sale here and there. Also, some debit card processing will include electronic checks. This allows people who are wary of electronic transfers to write a paper check, but you, as the seller, can cause the paper check to create an immediate withdrawal from the purchaser's bank account. In that way, you do not take the risk of the check bouncing.

As for the mechanics of accepting credit cards, check with your bank first. But don't settle for the bank's deal without checking other sources of "merchant processing." You'll find that the fees vary somewhat, depending on the volume of business that you will generate for the merchant processor, the average size of your sale, and other factors. Do check out the processor on these points:

+ The fee schedule.

+ How soon the proceeds of the credit card charges are deposited in your bank account.

+ What you can do to reduce fees.

+ How other businesses have fared using this processor (ask for references).

+ Whether the processor handles debit cards and paper checks.

Also note that when customers use their debit cards with pin numbers, the fee is substantially less than if they use debit cards as credit cards (that's when they sign credit card documents, even though they're using debit cards). Be sure to check this out before you sign with a merchant processor.

Factoring

In some industries and product lines, credit cards just don't do it. For instance, it's quite usual for the manufacturer of garments to extend liberal terms to a retail store or store chain. That's because the garment manufacturer wants stores to stock up on winter clothes in July and on summer clothes in January, so the manufacturer will offer terms that allow for payment sometime after delivery of the merchandise, when the retailer has sold some of the merchandise and has the cash to pay for it.

Obviously, extending these credit terms puts a real strain on the manufacturer's cash flow. It could ask, of course, for all the additional funds from the bank. But, as we discussed before, banks generally want securities. What can the manufacturer offer to the bank for security? Its biggest asset at this point is the accounts receivable from the retailers. Sometimes, banks will loan funds secured by an intangible asset such as accounts receivable. But if a banker has to repossess that asset, it's obviously a difficult task, because it puts the bank in the position of having to collect the accounts receivable. Also, accounts receivable are an evaporating asset. That is, they must be collected when due. As retail stores go out of business or change hands, it becomes increasingly difficult to collect from them. In other words, it takes a specialist to handle this type of financing.

That's what gave rise to the factoring industry. Factors are specialists in financing based on accounts receivable. They make a business of buying the accounts receivable from manufacturers and distributors for some figure that is less than the amount of the receivable. The factor then collects that receivable when due, pocketing as profit the difference between what it paid for the receivable and what it collects.

The Rippedshirt Manufacturing Company (RSM) manufactured pre-ripped shirts for those who wanted to protect their privacy by appearing to be destitute while still wearing new, expensive clothing. In August it shipped its line of fur-lined ripped shirts to its 100 dealers and sent them all invoices for $10,000 each, due on January 30 of the next year. RSM incurred costs and expenses of $800,000 to manufacture the shirts, and, because it was a small operation, that had drained the bank account and had tapped out the line of credit at the bank.

In order to have funds to continue operations, RSM turned to the Moremoney Factoring Company. It purchased the $1,000,000 of accounts receivable from RSM for $900,000, so it would have a profit of $100,000 if and when it collected all of the accounts receivable. Unfortunately, four of the stores went out of business and declared bankruptcy between August and January, so Moremoney collected only $960,000. That was still $60,000 more than the $900,000 it paid RSM for the accounts.

Everyone gained in this deal. The manufacturer received immediate funds and was rid of the collection hassle; the factor did net a few thousand after all expenses; and the retailers had merchandise to sell well before the season.

When You Extend Credit Yourself

Not all credit sales can be handled by credit cards or factors. If you are manufacturing railroad locomotives, you can hardly expect that the CEO of the railroad will stop at your shop, hand you his MasterCard, and drive the engine home.

Big Products and/or Large Customers

Obviously, large customers and large (expensive) products deserve special handling. If this is your type of business, or you get into this type of business, you should have a carefully drawn contract with the customer. The contract could include clauses that require the purchaser to make an initial deposit and continue to make progress payments during the length of the construction of the product. Certainly, you need a qualified attorney to draw up a contract and you should discuss your contract with your banker, anticipating any possible need for interim financing from the bank.

Suppose you have tied up all of your working capital in the manufacturing and assembling of large, expensive products, such as locomotives. In order to continue operations, you desperately need your cash out of this inventory. Because the

Baghdad Railroad Company wants immediate delivery of two locomotives, you make a deal that involves a cut-rate price. This provides little profit but keeps the cash flow going so you can remain in business. However, the Baghdad Railroad has similar cash flow problems and demands 90-day terms. That is, your invoice for the locomotives would not be due to be paid until 90 days after delivery. That is of little help to your immediate cash needs!

What can you do? Given the situation in Baghdad at this writing, you might convince the U. S. Government to either buy the locomotives from you and provide them to the railroad as part of the reconstruction of Iraq or to guarantee the payment of the debt by the Baghdad Railroad. Either way, you'll still wait for your money. But by getting our government involved and committed to eventual payment, you are in a much better position to take all the documentation to your banker and seek a loan for the amount of your invoice.

In actual practice, you should discuss your impending need for a loan before releasing products to buyers or becoming involved in the frustrations of dealing with the government.

When you are dealing with large, well-rated companies, or state and federal governments, the credit risk is not the ability of the customer to pay, but your ability to wend your way through the bureaucracy and the payment procedures of the customer. Be sure you understand the procedures and the paperwork that you will have to submit before you sell products or services to this type of customer. At the very least, even if the sale is for only a few dollars, be sure you receive a purchase order or at least a purchase order number before letting go of your goods.

In the case of large nongovernment entities, you also need to heed the previous "well-rated" comment. Remember that companies that are well regarded and pay their bills can suddenly change. At this writing, Enron, WorldCom, and Global

Crossings fall into this category. Protect yourself against losses such as suppliers to these companies have incurred. The bond ratings of reporting agencies, such as Standard & Poor's, may give you a clue. The Standard & Poor's rating book is available in larger libraries, and what the ratings mean is set forth in the book. Another source of information that may be even better is Dun & Bradstreet reports. They do cost some money, but can save thousands in credit losses. These reports can give you insight into the financial condition of the company and may offer some indication of how others find their payment history. Your banker may also have information that will be helpful in evaluating whether you should make sales to a large corporation. At the very least, he or she should be able to help you ferret out the most important information from the Dun & Bradstreet report. Note that Dun & Bradstreet also reports on small and medium companies, although their reports may not be as comprehensive as for those companies that are publicly held and, therefore, must publish financial information.

As an aside, you can also subscribe to a Dun & Bradstreet service that will provide you their report on your business periodically. If you and your business have good credit, subscribing to the service is well worth it. Making sure there are no errors in this report will ensure that you can buy on credit, which is a definite contribution to cash flow.

A similar category is those companies that have to declare bankruptcy but still continue operating much as usual under a "Chapter 11" organization. Selling anything but orders of very small dollar amounts to companies in bankruptcy takes special care. Normally, if you sell to such an entity after the bankruptcy court has accepted the bankruptcy petition, you become a preferred creditor and will be paid ahead of those who were left holding the bag when the company declared bankruptcy. However, the bankruptcy law is tricky and, at this writing, there is the bill in Congress to change much of it. Therefore, the only reasonable advice about this category of customer is to retain a bankruptcy attorney who can walk you through the risk and required paperwork needed to successfully sell to and collect from a bankrupt company.

Bonded Customers

When you sell goods and services for major construction projects, your credit evaluation may be done for you. Usually, the owner of the project will require that contractors on the job be bonded. What does that mean? The bonding company (often an insurance company) has checked out the credit of the contractors and has bonded them. The bond specifies that if the contractor fails to complete the job, or fails to pay for materials used on the job, the bonding company will pay for completion and pay the bills. The important thing to know here is that there is a time limit within which any claim for payment from the bonding company must be made. If you sell to customers who fit this description, be sure you get such information from them as the name of their bonding company and their file number, and from the bonding company, obtain the information as to how and when claims must be filed. And watch the "when"— suppliers and subcontractors have lost millions of dollars because someone neglected to inform the bonding company of unpaid invoices within a specified time limit.

Lien Rights

State laws vary, but generally anyone who provides goods and services to a parcel of real estate, a vehicle, boat, airplane, or other type of property, and does not get paid for the service or product, has lien rights against the property. Again, time is of the essence, for there is a period during which your claim for the property must be filed with the court. The first time you file such a claim, it would be a good idea to hire an attorney to walk you through the procedure. Thereafter, you probably can file the paperwork yourself.

Hard-Nosed Collections

An account receivable has an air of uncertainty about it. You know that a customer has always paid on time, but you don't know for certain if he or she will continue to pay on time. Situations change, luck changes, and if you sell to businesses, they commonly change owners and/or management. An experienced credit manager will tell you that the likelihood of collecting your bills declines with each passing day that they go unpaid. However, there are several things you can do to increase the likelihood that you will be paid—and paid on time.

Cash Discount for Quick Payment

Many companies, particularly those that sell to other businesses, such as contractors, permit their customers to subtract a percentage of the total from the invoice amount if they pay quickly. Should you include such a cash discount in your terms? This is an age-old question to which there is really no good answer. What you are doing is giving up the discount amount to collect your money in 10 instead of 30 days. If you're offering a 2 percent discount, that amounts to an annual rate of about 36 percent. That's expensive, but it does mean you are more likely to get your money, and more likely to receive it before other people, who do not give discounts, receive theirs. So how much is a bird in the hand worth? As the experts say, the later an invoice is scheduled to be paid, the less likely it will be paid, so the high interest costs may be well worth it.

As to what terms you should offer, that will depend on several factors. This list is not all-inclusive, but it will help in your decision making:

- ✦ Do you have the resources (as money in the bank) to be able to wait for your money?

- ✦ What, generally, are the terms offered by the competitors in your industry?

✦ If you're already in business, what are your present terms? Abrupt changes may prompt loyal customers to check with your competitors.

✦ If you offer cash discounts, would it still be profitable if most customers took advantage of the discount by paying within the specified time?

✦ Some people pay very promptly whether or not a cash discount is offered. Would offering one increase the number of people who pay promptly? If not, you may only be giving money away by offering it.

Whatever your terms are, it is important that your customers or clients understand those terms at the time they agree to use your services or purchase your product, and that they understand that you expect payment when due. To that end, terms should be clearly stated on the order form, contract, or engagement letter that the customer signs.

Make Your Terms Clear and Understandable

A sort of shorthand, such as "Terms: 2/10 n30" on your invoice does let us know that you have terms, but for many people, the shorthand is gibberish. So spell out those terms as, "Take a 2-percent cash discount if you pay within ten days from date of invoice, otherwise pay the net amount within 30 days from the date of the invoice." Such detail is hard to misunderstand. Of course, there are other terms that can be spelled out, such as "net 30" means "the invoice is due within 30 days from the date of the invoice." If you spell out your terms, instead of using a shorthand, you literally can specify almost any terms you can dream up. (Don't forget that "cash on delivery" is an option.) In this computer age, it takes no more effort to program the computer to spell out the terms than to print the shorthand.

Displaying the Age of the Account on Monthly Statements

Most of us have received a statement[1] from a business, and on the bottom of the statement are several boxes usually labeled as follows: "current," "30 days," "60 days," and "90 or more days." In each box is a portion of the total balance due. How much goes in each box is determined by the billing date of the invoice that fits that age.

In the struggle to keep the No-Hole Doughnut Shop alive, Ralph found that he was unable to pay all the charges for the flour that he purchased. On October 31, he received a monthly statement from the flour company, which listed his unpaid invoices as follows:

Date	Amount
Jul 10	$300
Jul 20	200
Aug 15	400
Sept 5	250
Sept 18	200
Oct 10	100
Total due	$1,450

Across the bottom of this statement, the aging would be printed:

Current	30 to 60 days	60 to 90 days	90+ days	Total
$100	$450	$400	$500	$1,450

Of course, this aging will not be much help in collecting from the customer who is one step away from the bankruptcy court. But for other customers, it does serve to remind them that their account is getting past due. Most people realize that such a condition may end up on a credit reporting agency's report and will diminish their ability to obtain credit from lenders and suppliers. At least, it provides you or your credit manager with information as to who needs to receive a phone call, letter, or other collection effort.

The Collection Routine

The important part about collections is the necessity to stay on top of this task. If your terms are "invoice due in 10 days," you need to start collection efforts in 15 days. (This allows for mail delay and other reasonable excuses.) For some businesses, this schedule may be appropriate:

✦ Start with the usual polite "reminder" letter that may start out with a simple "did you overlook?" or "did you forget?"

✦ Ten days later, send a stronger message.

✦ In another 10 days, send a really mean letter that might include a threat of legal action.

There are some sample collection letters in Appendix C, but please do not use them verbatim. You will need to temper them for the type of business you're in and the type of customer you have. For instance, if you have only a few large customers, writing form letters would not be the way to handle collections. Presumably, in that situation, each customer is important, so a personal phone call or even a visit to the customer may be a better collection method. In a two-way conversation you may be able to discern what is causing the slow payment and take corrective action.

On the other hand, if you have many small customers, form collection letters are the most expedient way to handle collections. It certainly is not cost-effective to take time to telephone, let alone visit, 1,000 people, each of whom owes you $14.95.

If it's appropriate for your type of business and type of customer, be sure to make it easy for the delinquent customer to pay. Specifically, include the opportunity to provide his or her credit card account number and expiration date. The credit card processing fee is well worth the ability to transfer your collection problem to the credit card company. If the customer is maxed out on his or her credit cards, try for a postdated check. Sometimes a series of postdated checks is preferable, because the first check should be dated just a few days in the future, and you'll find out right away if the checking account is still open and if there may be enough money in the customer's checking account to cover the checks he or she has written.

Sometimes, you will run into the type of customer who always waits until he receives your third collection letter (threatening legal action) before he sends a check. If you have customers like that, take the time to at least call them and discuss the problem, pointing out that you cannot afford to wait many weeks for your money and that, unless their payment history improves, you will have to insist on payment in advance (C.O.D.).

Once you realize you have a serious delinquency situation in an account receivable, try to obtain a signed note from the customer. That serves to help remove any argument as to the quality of goods or services the customer received and may strengthen your position in legal proceedings. If you can get your debtor to pledge some collateral (truck, boat, airplane, artwork, whatever), so much the better. If collateral is a possibility, have your lawyer help you with the documentation.

The final step is to drag your debtor into court. Should you represent yourself or your company or should you engage an attorney? Consider doing both. If the amount is relatively small, pursue the collection yourself in small claims court. (Most jurisdictions have such a court, but the maximum dollar amount that can be heard in such a court varies by state, so inquire about that locally with your attorney or the clerk of the court.) If the amount is large and/or you'll have to endure the formalities of a higher court, put your lawyer to work. If your market is such that you have a lot of small accounts, some of whom don't pay, gather up several deadbeat files, take them to the court clerk, and try to schedule all of them to be heard on the same day. That's about the only way to handle a bunch of small accounts.

The alternative, of course, is to consider it not worth the time to pursue them and write them off as bad debts. But before you do that, analyze how much more business you have to do to survive that write-off. In other words, if you write off $1,000 of bad accounts, and your profit margin is 20 percent, you will have to increase sales by $5,000 to regain the cash represented by the bad debts.

After you have obtained a judgment against your debtor, look through your file on that former customer for any indication of assets he or she has that may be attached and sold to satisfy the debt. Again, if the amount is large, let your attorney handle it. If it's relatively small, check with the clerk of the court about the procedure.

Then there is the case of a slow-payment history by a customer caused by reasons other than the customer's cash flow:

> I once worked in the credit department of an electrical supply distributor. We had a customer who delayed payment until he was seriously delinquent. We wondered what the problem was and telephoned him. He admitted that he was delaying payment intentionally; he withheld payment because he wanted to receive all of our collection letters, so he could use those letters in his business to send to his customers! To solve that problem, we simply sent him a complete file of our standard collection letters, and thereafter he always paid promptly!

And lastly, a minor aid in collections that is important with retail customers: Enclose a return envelope (without postage). Disorganized individuals tend to lose invoices and reminders before they can locate an envelope, so avoid that excuse. Also provide the Internet address where your customers can pay online, if that is their preference and you are able to process electronic payments.

Automating Cash Receipts

You can automate collecting and depositing money if your volume warrants it. Bank lockboxes and sweep accounts are two methods that are easily available.

Lockboxes:
Turn Receivables Into Cash Faster

Have you noticed that when you create your federal income tax forms, the IRS provides two addresses to which you can mail the forms? One address is for those who are not sending a check with their return, the other address is for those who are sending a check. Why two addresses? Because the IRS is an enthusiastic user of lockboxes.

Essentially, the lockbox is an address at a bank. The IRS, and almost any business (probably including yours), can have a bank set up a lockbox procedure for them. Checks to the lockbox are processed almost immediately upon receipt, starting the travel of the check through the clearing system far earlier than would be the case when the business receives check, records its receipt, perhaps photocopies the check, then makes up the deposit ticket and hand-carries the deposit to the bank. If that person arrives at the bank late in the day, the clearing process does not start until the next day.

This lockbox procedure also enhances the internal control of your company. That is, the people who open the mail, remove checks, and deposit them in the bank are completely separate from those who record the receipt in your books. The money receivers and those who record the receipt of funds are separate entities, so the opportunity for an employee to siphon off some of your hard-earned funds is non-existent. (For more on internal control, see Appendix B.)

Lockboxes work best for those who receive large checks and want to have cleared funds as soon as possible, as well as those who receive a large volume of small checks and want the efficiency of the bank processing. Your needs in the handling of receipts may be unusual, so if you find your bank cannot handle your needs, talk to other banks because they may offer the services you require. In any event, think about the enhanced internal control as you review the fees the bank will charge for this lockbox service.

The Sweep: Let the Bank Pay You for a Change

Consider how you would like this service from your bank: Every evening, when you return home, you throw your extra folding money and change on the floor of your living room. In a little while, your banker comes by with a broom and dustpan, *sweeps* up your money, takes it to the bank, and puts it in your savings account. It remains there, earning interest until you need it. And when you do need it, all you have to do is write a check, whether or not there are funds in your checking account. The account will not be overdrawn, because the bank will automatically transfer cash from your savings account to your checking account.

Well, the banker will not actually come by your house. In fact, he or she won't do anything except to set this program up for you. But the bank's computer will look at your checking account each night and *sweep* the excess cash into an interest-bearing account, where it remains until you need it. Then you obtain that money by writing a check, which the bank will cover with funds from your interest-bearing account. When interest rates are high, this can be an appealing service. So, although at this writing the rates are historically low, keep this in mind for future times when interest rates go up. Of course, like any bank service, you need to investigate the fees and compare the fees for the service against the benefits of the service. (Chapter 2 has more about bank fees.)

Summary of Accounts Receivable

Accounts receivable can be a cash generator or a cash drag. Be cautious in extending credit and be aggressive in collecting payment.

Do

☑ Contract others to handle your credit department functions. (Use credit cards and/or factors.)

☑ Obtain pertinent credit reports on customers—new and old. Remember that just because your prospective customer is a large company doesn't mean you will be paid promptly.

☑ If you do extend credit, set up routines to bill promptly and follow up with collection procedures on a schedule.

Don't

☒ Neglect this area of your business. Turn sales into cash as quickly as possible.

Sell Assets to Raise and Conserve Cash

If your assets include used machinery, equipment, or vehicles, or other assets, such as stocks and bonds, turn them into cash by selling them. You may think idle machinery and vehicles are worthless, but others may see value in them and pay real money for them.

Sale of Personal Assets

The cranky riding mower and the old car that might be (but isn't) a collectable are both sources of some cash. Should you advertise these items in the paper and on the Internet? Both of those methods take time. If you run your own business or are in the process of starting one, your time may be better spent in selling your product or service than in selling miscellaneous items out of your basement. Make a couple of phone calls to people who deal in used items you'd like to get rid of to determine if they would pay you anything for them. Even if there isn't much money to be had, it will take some of the clutter out of your life, and that's a plus. Also investigate the possibility of making donations of these items to a charity. (See the discussion of tax implications in the following section.)

Do you have stocks, bonds, mutual funds, real estate, and other investments that can easily be sold through a broker? Should you sell these items? It depends on how critical it is that you raise cash immediately. If your investments are returning an income to you that is a higher rate of return than the bank would charge you for borrowing the funds, you may be better off to use investments as security and borrow the funds. If your investments are paying you less, you may be better off selling them—but see the following section on tax considerations.

Also, don't overlook any life insurance policies that have cash value. Although you could borrow from the insurance company, using the cash value as security, that procedure creates a loan that would be paid off by the proceeds from the life insurance, so the proceeds would go to the insurance company rather than to your family. If you convert the life insurance policy to a term life insurance policy and withdraw the cash value, you will have the cash *and* continue the protection, in the event of your death, for the face amount of the policy.

> Ben was about to open his own shop for the repair of automobiles. Because he had a family, he would need to have life insurance protection for their welfare should something unfortunate happen to him. He currently has a $300,000 life insurance policy on which he pays a premium of $200 a month, and the cash

value of his policy, at present, is $100,000. He could borrow that amount from the insurance company and use those funds to start his business. However, if he should die, the insurance company would generate the $300,000 proceeds from the policy, deduct $100,000 to pay off the loan, and Ben's family would receive only $200,000.

In seeking an alternative, Ben finds that he can purchase a renewable term life insurance policy for a premium of only $50 per month. Therefore, by cashing in his present policy and purchasing the term policy, he extracts $100,000 in cash from the policy, lowers his monthly outgo by $150 per month, and his family would receive the full $300,000 in the event of his demise. Ben should buy the new policy before canceling the old in case any medical problems crop up that could make him ineligible for the new term policy. Also, he should make certain the policy is renewable, without medical restrictions, to at least age 65. (These figures are for illustration only. Results of this procedure for you will vary depending on the age of the insured and other factors.)

Tax Considerations in Sales of Assets

This is not a tax book, but any time you sell anything you own, you need to be able to estimate the net cash flow you will receive from that sale. *Net cash flow* is what is left over after you pay expenses of the sale. Included in those expenses is the income tax, so it is important to estimate that expense as well.

If you sell your old riding lawn mower or personal automobile, the chances are that you will sell those items for less than you paid for them, so there would be no tax due on the proceeds of those sales. (If you should happen to sell an item for more than you paid for it, you could end up with a tax bill on part of the money from that sale.)

If you sell stocks, bonds, and mutual funds, there could be some income tax due on the proceeds of those sales. The tax amount depends on whether you had a gain or loss and on the period of time you owned those items. The good news is that, if you owned those assets for more than a specific period, you would pay at a lower long-term capital gain rate. The bad news is that, if you had a loss on that sale, you would be able to deduct (from ordinary income) only part of the loss in the current year.

Other than your residence, if you sell real estate that you rented to tenants, the computation of the tax becomes complicated. That's because the depreciation that you have claimed over the years will reduce the basis of the property, which means that the gain on the sale of the property will be greater. This computation is further complicated by the fact that part of your gain will be taxed at ordinary income tax rates and part may be taxed at capital gain rates. However, if the real estate you sell is unimproved land, there is no depreciation to confuse the calculation of gain.

The sale of used business equipment is somewhat similar to the sale of rental real estate. The depreciation that has been claimed on the equipment reduces the basis of the equipment, so the gain on the equipment is greater than you might expect.

In this computation of tax effects, you may find that donating used equipment to your favorite charity may actually generate more cash. However, this is only true if you itemize your deductions on your individual income tax return. There is one exception to this itemizing requirement: If you do business within a "C" corporation, you will not be concerned with what you can deduct on your individual income tax return, because the corporation deducts the charitable contribution. However, there are other limits on corporate charitable contributions.

Whatever you do in the way of selling assets, pay particular attention to the rules regarding sale of assets that are held within a retirement plan, such as a 401(k) or an IRA. If you withdraw the proceeds of asset sales from the plan and you're younger than 59 ½, you could be subject to a penalty for early withdrawal. In addition, the entire amount of withdrawal is subject to a penalty for early withdrawal. (In certain circumstances, that magic no-penalty age is 55, so check your circumstances with your tax advisor.) In addition, the entire amount of withdrawal is subject to income taxes at ordinary income tax rates.

Obviously if you have several investments that you want to sell in order to finance your business, it takes careful tax planning as far as *what* to sell and *when* to sell if the tax bite is to be minimized. You can try to work this out yourself, but I strongly urge you to have an accountant, who specializes in tax matters, review your computations before you proceed on a selling plan.

I apologize for the complexity of this short discussion of the income tax effect. If it sounds complicated, that's because it is. If this discussion included all factors that go into planning asset sales to minimize taxes, this would become a book on taxes rather than on cash flow. So, if this section convinces you to seek more information and professional tax help, it has met its purpose.

Sale of Business Assets

Most of the discussion about selling personal assets applies also to business assets, but there are other considerations relevant to just business assets. You may have equipment that you use at times but not very frequently, and that might be costing you money. For instance, you may have a printing press that you use once a month to generate a newsletter to customers. Would you be better off selling the printing or duplicating equipment and subcontracting the job of printing and mailing the newsletter? In order to determine this, you'll have to get an estimate of the current cash value of the equipment, an estimate of the current cost of the clerical help that is used in producing the newsletter, and an estimate of what it would cost to have it done outside of your company. After you have done the calculations, you may find that it is more economical to contract with a specialized company to perform this part of your operation.

Examples of functions that can often be performed more economically by others include printing and mailing (as we discussed), payroll preparation and payroll tax reporting, all the functions of the human resources department, employee benefits administration, and, of course, cleaning and maintenance of your office and other spaces.

Summary of Finding
Cash in Selling Assets

The bottom line is this: If you're not using something, sell it and put the resulting cash to work.

Do

☑ Write up an inventory of idle equipment and other stuff. Then sell it, unless you can come up with a very good reason to keep it.

☑ Balance the sales effort against what you could be doing otherwise with your time. Sell at a reduced price to save time, unless the item is worth a high amount.

☑ Calculate the tax bite on the proceeds of selling each type of asset. If you don't need to sell all of the assets, sell those that will result in lowest tax (as in the case of securities).

Don't

☒ Try to calculate the tax effect of sales when significant money is involved without professional help or review.

CHAPTER 2

Where to Save Cash

The most obvious way to save cash is to not spend it. Of course, that's an oversimplification. Every business has some expenses that must be paid, even if they're only rent and a telephone bill, but most businesses have many more types of required expenses. If you're plagued by the problem of not having enough cash at the end of month, you might think it wise to consider all expenses as existing in a common pot and decide that every expense will have to be cut by some percentage. That sounds as though it will work, but it's not practical. Some expenses can be cut drastically and some, unfortunately, hang around at the same level they always have.

I wish we could make up an all-inclusive list of which expenses can be easily slashed and which ones cannot be reduced. Yes, we could do that for a specific company, but we can't make up a general list, because the nature of each expense will vary from business to business. For instance, a sole paperwork pusher such as an accountant, lawyer, or insurance agent could reduce rent expense by simply moving his or her operations into a spare room in the home. For the individual who owns the neighborhood gas station, that's an impossible solution. In other words that person is stuck with an expense that cannot be reduced. (Of course, there is an outside chance of reducing it by negotiation with the landlord, but that would be unlikely unless you're in a decaying area.) So this discussion of how to save on some of those expenses will start out with areas where real savings may be made and end up with those areas where there may be little or no savings for many businesses.

Accounts Payable

Accounts payable procedures can run the gamut from a "pay the bill as soon as it arrives" system to a "put-out-the-fire" system. (The put-out-the-fire system can be defined as a system of paying some bills whenever there is some cash, and the bills that probably will be paid are from those suppliers who have yelled for payment the loudest. Somewhere in between is a "the bills get paid when they are due—no later, and no sooner" system. Let's look briefly at each system.

The Pay-the-Bill-as-Soon-as-it-Arrives System

This is a system that, for many individuals, works very well. For those who are employed in a steady job, with a constant income stream, paying a bill as soon as it arrives certainly avoids incurring service charges for late payments, some of which, as in the case of credit cards, can be onerous. However, that can be a dangerous procedure for a business. All businesses are subject to fluctuations in sales and those fluctuations are often brought about by circumstances beyond the managers' control. Unless a business is cash rich and has far more cash than it could possibly need for operations, it is wiser to keep cash in the bank for unforeseen emergencies. That is not to say that any bills or invoices should be paid later than the due date, but there is little to be derived from early payment. (Of course, there are exceptions: If the business that rendered the invoice is in a position to do you favors—as in providing scarce materials—then early payment may be worthwhile.) Here's an example of this policy:

Betty owned the Betty's Crumbly Bread & Biscuits Baking Company. She started the business two years ago, and it had grown rapidly. Last year, she moved to a commercial building and hired the first of six employees who came on board. When she started the business, she baked by herself in her home kitchen and sold her product to a few friends and neighbors. Because she had good personal credit, she was able to establish an account with her major supplier, the Fabulously Fertile Flour Company. She continued the policy she had always had with her personal bills; that is, she paid each bill on the day it arrived in her mail, regardless of when it was due or what it was for (supplies, utilities, taxes, rent, and so on).

And she went even further into check writing. During the late winter and early spring business was terrific. Valentine's Day, Easter, and other holidays provided incentives for customers to buy bakery products. During the same period, she received an offer from the company that provided her fire and burglar alarms. If she paid three years in advance for service, she could receive a 10 percent discount. She jumped at the chance to save some money and wrote a check for the three years of service. Then her insurance company covered her property and liability insurance with three-year policies and billed her for the premiums. The insurance company's invoice included an offer to allow quarterly or annual payments, but Betty chose to pay the entire bill and "get it out of the way."

The Put-out-the-Fire System

There are many situations in which, if you're not organized, you pay dearly. Accounts payable is certainly one such area.

Later, in the middle of summer, business was slow because most people consumed soda and potato chips at the beach rather than cakes and pies in their family rooms. Also, the highway department was repaving the street in front of the bakery. One fateful day in July, Betty received the usual weekly bill from the Fabulously Fertile Flour Company. She started to write a check to pay it but noticed that the bank balance was insufficient to cover the check. So for the first time, the flour invoice was set aside. With the low sales volume, it was several days before there was enough money to pay the invoice, as there was a payroll that had to be met first. When she paid the flour invoice, it was 10 days late—a serious transgression in the food business. In order to pay it, she had to set the electric bill aside to be paid whenever there were enough funds available.

By the end of September, she had fallen so far behind in her bill paying that the Fabulously Fertile Flour Company was requiring cash on delivery, the electric company was threatening to cancel service, and two months' worth of payroll taxes due the IRS remained unpaid. Betty laid off three of her six employees, but it was a little late. In the middle of October, the bank repossessed the mixers and ovens it had financed, so Betty was out of business and would probably have to file bankruptcy.

The Right Way

What could Betty have done differently? For starters, she could have ignored the "good deal" that the alarm company offered her. Sure, she saved 10 percent, but that's over a 3-year period. That means she earned substantially less than 10 percent per year on the money that she loaned the alarm company by paying in advance. Similarly, when she paid her insurance premiums for three years in advance, she loaned her money to the insurance company at a zero interest rate. If she had paid the alarm company and the insurance company only what was due for each calendar quarter, she might have had enough in the bank to weather the hard times she suffered in the summer.

Of course, she could have also laid off some employees sooner. Beyond that, she could have projected her cash inflows and outflows during the slow months and made arrangements to weather them. For instance, she could have asked her flour supplier for some special terms that would let her pay a portion of her bill in the November and December holiday seasons when receipts would be more than adequate. She might also have negotiated major change in payment terms with the bank or established a line of credit to provide the funds needed during this slow period. It's important to note that suppliers, banks, and finance companies will extend special payment terms only to businesses that are current in their obligations. In other words, instead of taking the time to write checks every day, Betty should have used her time to set up a system that would foresee the predicament before she was in trouble and be in a position to take corrective action.

What Betty did accomplish was to exemplify both extremes: She started with the compulsive pay-a-bill-as-soon-as-it-arrives and in ended with a helter-skelter "put-out-the-fire-system."

Yes, with all the bills that arrive at a business, scheduling payments may seem like a time-consuming task one would like to avoid. But those who avoid it may end up the way Betty did. If you have accounting software so that you can keep track of your business and prepare financial statements and tax returns, it may well contain a system for monitoring accounts payable. If you utilize a bookkeeping service to create these necessary records for tax return preparation, that means that your basic accounting records are off-site, and trying to keep accounts payable records off site at a bookkeeping service is awkward and time-consuming. A better method is to set up an accounts payable monitoring system on a spreadsheet that can be kept either on a computer or even with a pencil and paper. (There's a suggested spreadsheet system discussed on pages 63 and 64, or you may prefer to have your accountant set up a system designed especially for your needs.)

Remember that accounts payable do not exist in a vacuum. Managing them requires input from the whole business picture, including cash generated from sales, necessary purchases of merchandise and materials that will be consumed by the sales, and nearly all other facets of your business.

However, if you are in a mom-and-pop-sized business, you may be able to get away with a simple accounts payable system. Here are some suggestions and things to avoid:

The Dated File System

Set up a file folder for each day of the month for at least two months, or you can buy an accordion file from the office supply store that has 31 slots in it. File the invoice in the slot for the day on which you should pay it—and remember to check it every day. Although this basic system will get the job done (if you have the cash available), it has several shortcomings. These are:

✦ Without a lot of pencil pushing, you won't know how much cash you need on a certain day until you open the file for that day and all the days leading up to it.

✦ If you are looking for a certain vendor's invoice and can't remember when it's due, you have to look through all the daily files.

✦ The system takes care of only what you have already purchased and agreed to pay for. If sales are expected to dramatically increase, as in a seasonal business, this system will not project the increased need for cash to pay bills for the higher purchases and other expenses.

In other words, all this system does is organize your check writing.

The Spreadsheet System (Laying it out Visually)

This system allows you to look at the whole picture of your accounts payable and other cash needs, but otherwise has the same drawbacks as the file-folder system. It does make a good supplement to the file-folder system, because on the spreadsheet you can insert estimates of payments you know you will have to make—before you know the exact amount.

Table 2-1 on page 64 is a suggestion for setting this up as either a paper or electronic spreadsheet. Make up and copy a blank form (without the numbers) for the current and next month. Rather than making a separate column for each month, I suggest inserting the dates of each Friday in the month plus the 15th of the month. Friday isn't a magic day, but I use it because it's payday, and payday is a major disbursement day. Use whatever day is your payday for payment dates. The 15th of the month is the day of the month on which you should deposit payroll taxes in a bank or remit them electronically to the IRS. If you wait until the 16th, you're in line for a penalty!

No-Hole Doughnut Shop

Schedule of Disbursements to be Made for Accounts Payable, Payroll, and Taxes for the Month of: May 2003

Day of month	2	9	15	16	23	30
Recurring disbursements						
Rent	$	$	$	$	$	$ 3,000
Computer leasing company		225				
Electric company				825		
Telephone Company					125	
Wireless phone company					50	
Insurance premiums—general liability		200				
Insurance premiums—casualty		150				
Insurance premiums—workers comp.		100				
Payroll disbursements						
Net payroll	2,200	2,200		2,200	2,200	2,200
Unemployment insurance tax						25
Federal payroll taxes			2,500			
State payroll taxes			300			
Other disbursemeents						
Siftem Flour Company		800			1,000	
Sweeter Sugar Company		200			300	
Slippery Cooking Oil Company				400		300
Donut Box Company	300					
Window washing service	25	25		25	25	25
Totals	$2,525	$3,900	$2,800	$3,450	$3,700	$2,525

Table 2-1: System for keeping track of accounts payable due dates and amounts

If you know that you will have to pay an invoice by a certain date but have not yet received the invoice, pencil in an estimated amount. When you receive the invoice, change the temporary amount to the exact amount and recalculate the total for that date. (It's that recalculation that makes an electronic spreadsheet preferable to keeping track on paper. All electronic spreadsheets, such as Microsoft Excel, Corel QuattroPro, and IBM Lotus 1-2-3, will allow you to insert formulas for the column totals so they will update as you change the invoice amounts.)

Start controlling your payables with this basic procedure. As you become comfortable with it and it becomes part of your routine, extend it to be part of the whole cash flow planning scene described in Chapter 4.

Using Purchase Orders

If you have worked for the government or any large organization in an administrative job, you have faced the ordeal of purchase orders. Generally, they consist of a multipart form that requires approval by several people in order to buy a new pencil sharpener. Why do financial people insist on the use of purchase orders? Because they want to know how much money they will have to spend to pay for items that have already been ordered. That's also good information for a small-business person to have. If you have records that show that you have already ordered a $1-million printing press, you won't slip up and order another one for which you do not have the money or the credit line available. (Okay, I understand you will remember ordering $1-million machine— but will you remember ordering $500 worth of special paper?)

For your purchase order system, you don't need multipart forms. In fact, the only paper you need is a notebook with a couple of columns laid out in it. In the first column, list some numbers in order. (I like to start this type of list with a high number, such as 92764, so it will impress the supplier to whom I give that number.) In the second column, list the items you have ordered with a total amount of the order. Then, put that figure on the spreadsheet on which you keep your accounts payable. Of course, the best routine is to use the purchase order system in your accounting software, if it comes with one. Again, I stress that a purchase order system does not need to be fancy, such as one General Motors may use; it's just a tool. Don't buy the biggest hammer you can find, just buy the one that will pound in sixpenny nails.

Summary of Accounts Payable

A proper handling of accounts payable can result in significant savings for your business. The savings result from suggestions as follows:

Do

☑ Take cash discounts when offered by vendors. (See Appendix A for the computation of annual interest equivalents of cash discounts.)

☑ Get set up to make payments electronically, if you haven't already. That way you can make just-in-time payments without risking delays in the postal system.

☑ Keep some kind of record of what you have ordered and the resulting amount that will be due in the future.

Don't

☒ Rely on vendor statements to remind you of invoices that are due. Part of your accounts payable system should check for missing invoices that might go beyond the discount day or for missing payments you have made. (If you want a real nightmare, tie up your money in paying a large invoice twice.)

Reduce Inventory Costs

When we discuss inventory here, we're talking about that stock of goods that a business selling tangible goods will have to keep on hand. Specifically, the businesses are manufacturing, wholesale distributing, and retailing. A strictly service business won't have inventory except for a few supplies, such as office supplies. We'll cover that when we get to administrative expenses.

Forces That Affect Inventory

Essentially, inventory costs are driven by two opposing forces. One is the cost of keeping the merchandise on the shelf ready for the customer to buy. The other is the force of the market, which dictates that, insofar as possible, you have goods available when your customers are ready to buy. From a financial aspect, it would be cheaper to have zero inventory. From a marketing aspect, it would be advantageous to have a huge inventory of every conceivable item you might sell some day.

Financial Forces on Inventory (Costs)

The following list of inventory costs is not all-inclusive, as these costs will vary from industry to industry:

✦ The invoice cost of the product.

✦ Interest expense on the money you borrowed to purchase the inventory or the interest you could have earned on your own money if you had not invested it in inventory.

✦ The cost of storage space (room, shelving, etc.) in which to keep the inventory.

✦ The cost of shipping the merchandise to you, if the terms of the sales are that the buyer pays the shipping costs.

✦ Any costs incurred in assembling the merchandise.

✦ In a manufacturing environment, the cost of labor to fabricate and assemble the product, as well as supplies consumed in that manufacturing operation.

Market Forces on Inventory

Marketing considerations are more difficult to reduce to hard numbers. They can best be expressed as questions to which most answers will be a matter of opinion (or an educated guess or even a wild guess). Consider these:

✦ Will stocking obscure, hard-to-find items bring traffic—customers who will also purchase popular items that many competitors also stock? For instance, if a hardware store does not stock drill bits (average retail price of $3), it probably will not sell many $50 electric drills.

✦ Can you avoid stocking slow-moving merchandise by stocking and selling only popular items? That may be possible if you price your goods lower than your competitors, but it leaves questions of "How *much* cheaper?" and "Can you generate a net profit after lowering prices?"

Before we demonstrate how inventory can affect cash flow, there is a basic concept that's important in determining how much inventory you should have on your shelves. It's called *turnover*.

Inventory Turnover

For an illustration of this concept, suppose that you go into business as a street vendor of brooms, with very limited capital. Your capital allows you to buy only one broom from the broom wholesaler, which you do purchase. Then you stand on a nearby street corner hawking the broom. Eventually, someone buys it. In order to continue in business, you return to the wholesaler, buy another broom and return to your street corner. After someone buys that broom, you again return to the wholesaler, buy another broom, and so on. At the end of the day, you have repeated the process of buying and selling a broom 10 times. During the whole day, your total inventory was one broom. Even though there were 10 different brooms, you never had more than one broom in your hand (*on hand*). In inventory-speak, you had a turnover of 10.

The formula for the turnover rate is: *Divide the number of items sold during a period by the average inventory on hand during the period*. For instance, if you sell 10 left-handed monkey wrenches in one year, and you kept an inventory of five of those wrenches on hand, we would say that the inventory turned over twice.

If you want to sound like an accountant, substitute the word *units* for the word *items* in the formula. Accountants like to use "unit" because it allows them to compute an inventory of something like wheat; they picture a bushel of wheat as a unit of measure rather than an item. That's a minor concept, but there are more important ones.

If your shelves have three sizes of left-handed monkey wrenches (8 inches, 10 inches, and 12 inches), arriving at total turnover of all left-handed monkey wrenches is more complex. Because you probably didn't sell the same number of each size, you have a different turnover for each size. Computing a turnover for the whole class of left-handed monkey wrenches, using unit counts, gets into math that is higher than we want to use here. When you extend that to computing the turnover of inventory for the whole tool department or the entire store, determining which units were sold, and when, becomes an endless task. For this reason, turnover is usually expressed in dollars rather than units or items. The formula becomes the cost of the units sold divided by the dollar amount (at cost) of the average inventory. That is often simplified further by using the inventory at the end of the period (such as one year) as the divisor.

Some well-meaning soul may tell you that you have to resolve an inventory valuation challenge at this point. He or she proposes that there is a further complication here in determining the cost of the items in the inventory versus the cost of the items sold, if the price at which they were purchased fluctuated during the year. In other words, do you envision that the wrenches you purchased first were sold first or were they sold last? If we pursue this point, we'll be into a long discussion of *first-in, first-out* and *last-in, first-out* inventory methods. This is important for accountants when they compute profit on an income statement or tax return, but it does not change your cash flow. (What you paid for the wrenches is cash outflow regardless of whether that expenditure for wrenches increased inventory or is in the cost of the wrenches sold.) Therefore, we will leave that discussion for other books. I bring it up here only to point out that it does not directly affect cash flow. (There is some *indirect* effect because inventory valuation is part of the computation of income tax.)

There are two used-car lots in town that, with a few exceptions, are almost identical. Calvin's Classic Cars is on the corner of Main Street and Third Avenue; Andrea's Almost New Cars is at Main Street and Sixth Avenue. The cash flow of their operations during the year before last looks like Table 2-2. For simplicity, we'll assume that all sales are for cash and both entrepreneurs pay for the cars they buy, as well as all overhead expenses, with cash. As is obvious, the two used-car operations are identical except that Andrea sold (turned over) twice as many cars as did Calvin, and the result is that she put money ($230,000) in her pocket while Calvin was out $20,000. (See Table 2-2 on page 72.)

There were a couple of changes for the next year. Calvin decided to keep fewer cars in the inventory on his lot and specialize in finding cars that customers wanted. That meant his inventory was only 10 cars, and the interest on the money he borrowed to finance his inventory was cut in half. Andrea, on the other hand, decided she could better serve her customers if she had more cars in the inventory on her lot, so she maintained an inventory of 80 cars. This resulted in a higher interest expense for the financing of that inventory. Table 2-3 reflects this second year, and it's obvious that the difference in net cash flow between Calvin and Andrea was reduced to only $5,000. (See Table 2-3 on page 73.)

First Year

	Calvin's Classic Cars	Andrea's Almost New Cars
Sale price of car	$ 20,000	$ 20,000
Cost of car	$ 17,500	$ 17,500
No. of units sold	100	200
Average inventory (units)	20	20
Average inventory ($)	$ 350,000	$ 350,000
Interest rate, annual	20%	20%
Annual interest on average inventory	$ 70,000	$ 70,000
Overhead (rent, etc.)	$ 200,000	$ 200,000
Cash flow statement		
Cash from sales (100 cars)	$ 2,000,000	$ 4,000,000
Cash paid to purchase cars sold	1,750,000	3,500,000
Cash flow from sales	250,000	500,000
Cash outflow for expenses		
Interest expense	$ 70,000	$ 70,000
Overhead (rent, etc.)	200,000	200,000
Total outflow for expenses	270,000	270,000
Net cash inflow	$ (20,000)	$ 230,000

Table 2-2: First year of automobile sales

Second Year

	Calvin's Classic Cars	Andrea's Almost New Cars
Sale price of car	$ 20,000	$ 20,000
Cost of car	$ 17,500	$ 17,500
No. of units sold	100	200
Average inventory (units)	10	80
Average inventory ($)	$ 175,000	$ 1,400,000
Interest rate, annual, on borrowed funds	20%	20%
Annual interest on average inventory	$ 35,000	$ 280,000
Overhead (rent, etc.)	$ 200,000	$ 200,000
Cash flow statement		
Cash from sales (100 cars)	$ 2,000,000	$ 4,000,000
Cash paid to purchase cars sold	1,750,000	3,500,000
Cash flow from sales	250,000	500,000
Cash outflow for expenses		
Interest expense	$ 35,000	$ 280,000
Overhead (rent, etc.)	200,000	200,000
Total outflow for expenses	235,000	480,000
Net cash inflow	$ 15,000	$ 20,000

Table 2-3: Second year of automobile sales

How did that happen? Only three things changed: the inventory level, the inventory turnover, and the interest expense. The higher inventory level caused the higher turnover, and together they resulted in the high interest expense.

I admit that this example may be somewhat exaggerated, but its purpose is not to portray the used car business accurately, but to demonstrate the effect of inventory levels and turnover.

Opportunity Cost

Perhaps you're one of the fortunate few who have ample funds available and therefore invest your own money in inventory, so you pay no interest to the bank or finance company. That's great, but you still have an expense that's called *opportunity cost*. In the Calvin and Andrea example, instead of investing an additional $1,050,000 in her inventory, Andrea could have invested it in low-rated bonds (a risk similar to that of owning a business) and perhaps earned 12 percent without the effort and hassle of selling automobiles.

Just-in-Time Inventory Delivery

Please picture yourself back in the broom business, where you purchased one broom at a time and sold one broom at a time. That was the epitome of just-in-time inventory, because you repeatedly added one broom to your inventory just in time to sell it. Major manufacturers have honed this procedure to the point that many of their raw materials arrive at the plant just hours before they are needed. In fact, some automobile manufacturers have arranged for their major suppliers to build their factories or warehouses next to the automobile manufacturers' plants.

For a small business, it's difficult to convince the supplier to pick up and move its whole operation next to yours. However, you may be able to come close to this minimum inventory picture by conferring with your suppliers as to delivery service or, if they're some distance away, including the charges for airfreight in your negotiation.

Summary of Inventory

Be aware of the cost of tying your money up in inventory and consider these suggestions:

Do

☑ Stock enough inventory to meet most of your customers' needs.

☑ Be mindful of how important your business has become to your suppliers as your business has grown—you may have grown into a position where you can demand just-in-time deliveries.

☑ Check your inventory turnover ratio often (at least monthly).

☑ Ask suppliers for special terms (such as payment not due for 90 or 120 days) if seasonal factors require a buildup in inventory.

Don't

☒ Stock more inventory than you need.

☒ Think that you must produce or stock everything your customers may want. You can't be the sole source of everything.

☒ Hang on to old inventory until it is virtually worthless. If you make a wrong buying decision, sell the material or product for whatever you can get. (It is better that you, rather than a liquidator, get whatever cash can come from such a sale.)

Payroll Expense

If your business is, or will be, a one-person show, you obviously cannot cut expenses by downsizing. However, this section is still relevant because someday you may hire your first employee and many more thereafter. It's never too early to think about how you will compensate employees—how you set up a wage and salary policy can have good and bad consequences in later years.

The cost of keeping employees on board is one of the first things owners and top managers look at when it comes time to reduce cash outflows. This is to be expected as payroll makes up such a large part of the expense in most businesses. Despite being in the computer age, there hasn't been any reduction in the need for employees, although the nature of the needed employees has changed somewhat. (That is, the need is for employees with more skills and education.) Following is a rundown on approaches to the challenge of reducing payroll expense.

Reduce the Workforce

If your employees are relatively unskilled and easily replaced, and training takes little time, it may make sense to lay off some of them to reduce expense. Do this with the realization that you will incur some training costs, even for the most unskilled jobs, when times are better and you need more hands working in your business. Also remember that when you need these unskilled people in good times, it may be harder to find individuals who are reliable. Obviously, if you lay off management personnel, your training of new hires when times are better will incur much more expense. You may be able to solve some of this dilemma if you hang on to managers by using them for less skilled tasks and laying off the unskilled employees who formerly did those tasks. To make this work, you will have something of a sales job if you're to convince managers to accept this program. But it may be preferable to being unemployed, which might happen if your need to cut back is caused by a general recession.

Should you keep managers' salaries at their high levels? If you decide to, you are overpaying for the work accomplished, but saving future hiring and training costs to replace managers who you terminate. If you decide not to, you may have fewer trained managers.

Cut Working Hours

Cutting back the number of hours that hourly paid employees may work in a week may be doable if your cutback is something in the area of changing from 40 hours per week to 37 hours. If you plan ahead for such a curtailment of work and give employees some notice so they can plan their financial life, this may solve your expense-reduction challenge. It helps if, in this process, you explain the reasons for the curtailment of hours to the employees (for example, that business is slow, that a big contract did not materialize, or whatever else can be a good reason for the cutback).

Warning: Don't cut everyone's hours and take-home pay and then show up at the office in a brand new Lincoln Navigator!

However, if you need to do a drastic curtailment of hours, such as from 40 to 20 hours per week, you can rest assured that the employees will be looking for full-time employment elsewhere. The result may be that you are left with the more inefficient and unreliable employees while your competitors have hired the good ones. To avoid that result, take the bull by the horns and lay off the least desirable employees so *you* keep the good ones.

Obviously, cutting working hours for salaried employees, particularly at the management level, will generate the opposite to the desired effect unless you also cut salaries by some percentage. When it comes to top management—your "idea" people—cutting salaries may not be wise, for that action does not contribute to management motivation. (This is a strong reason to base much of management compensation on a bonus formula. When business is bad, they automatically get paid less. When managers figure out how to run the business more efficiently, they receive their bonuses again.) For these salaried employees, the next alternative may be preferable.

Demand More Work Per Employee Hour

This sounds like a good idea, but running shorthanded, thereby requiring more output per employee, can have various consequences. For instance, if an employee has customer contact, and the employee is pushed to complete numerous administrative tasks at the same time he or she is supposed to be helping customers, the friendliness and helpfulness to the customer may be seriously impaired. Have you ever sought help from a sales clerk in a large discount or warehouse store and found that the employees seem to be more pressured to stock shelves than really help a customer? If this is your store, put those highly paid managers to work training employees on how to work more efficiently, so that there is time to help the needy customer.

However, putting more pressure on clerical and administrative management employees can reduce payroll costs. Many of these people often have a "bookkeeper outlook." That is, every phase of their job should be organized, compartmentalized, and in balance. If a bookkeeper's records are out of balance by $12, he or she should be satisfied that there is not a $100,000 error one way and an offsetting error the other way of $99,988. One should ignore $12 and go on to other work. Requiring more work from this bookkeeper in limited time should accomplish that.

What Does an Employee Cost?

In deciding where, when, and how to cut employee costs, it helps to know what these costs are. Refer to the chart on pages 80 and 81.

Replace Employees With Contractors

If you know the total cost of an employee, you are in a position to ask outside contractors for a proposal to perform the same task as the employees, and then compare your present costs of an employee to the cost in the proposal from the contractor. For instance, you can contract with others to prepare your payroll reports and, indeed, be your whole human resources department. If your type of business calls for taking physical inventories at certain times, you can contract with an inventory service rather than using your own employees. And, of course, the manufacture or assembly of the product you sell may be performed by another manufacturer.

Calculating the Total Cost of an Employee	
Gross Pay	Pay earned before deductions.
Social Security	7.65% up to $87,000 of gross pay in 2003, then 1.45% of all in excess of that amount.
Unemployment Tax, Federal and State	Rate varies by state and employer layoff history. In most states, it is levied on only the first $7,000 of wages—most often the maximum is 6.2% of the first $7,000 or $434 per employee.
Workers' Compensation Insurance	Varies by nature of work of employee and type of industry.
Medical Insurance	Varies for multiple factors. Obtain quotes and check into group rates.
Pension Plan or 401(k) Matching	Employer costs vary, depending on the plan. Obtain figures from your plan consultant or sponsor.
Vacation and Holiday Cost	Generally 2 weeks' pay plus the taxes and other costs as above.

Calculating the Total Cost of an Employee (continued)	
Training	Length of training multiplied by the rate of pay. Add taxes, cost of instructor(s), instruction space (school room), etc.
Liability Insurance	Check your insurance policies. Payroll expense or the number of employees may be part of the computation of premium—particularly true for professional liability coverage.
Space, Tools, and Equipment to Enable Employee to Work	Use the rental value of the floor space and real depreciation of the equipment. (This may or may not be a fixed expense that will not go away if the employee is laid off.)
Human Resources Department Expense	Total cost of human resources department divided by number of employees.

* Where the actual figures for these costs are too difficult or expensive to obtain, make the best estimates possible.

This is a particularly important alternative in these days when it may be considerably less expensive to manufacture products offshore, but you really won't know unless you do a thorough analysis of your manufacturing, and the most important ingredient in that is the cost of employees engaged in the fabrication activity.

Understandably, you may have qualms about laying off long-term, loyal employees in order to utilize a less-expensive contractor. In this respect, there are two thoughts to bear in mind:

✦ Consider our highly competitive world economy. If you do not take measures to reduce your cash outflow, there won't be jobs (at your shop) for any of your long-term faithful employees.

✦ Do not overlook the possibility of converting an individual from employee to contractor status. This can well represent a reduction in costs for you without reducing the after-tax pay to the former employee, inasmuch as there are some tax breaks available to self-employed people that are not available to employees. But there is this major warning: In converting an employee to a subcontractor, be mindful of the Internal Revenue Service. It has confusing rules about who can be classified as a contractor instead of an employee, so seek professional advice before taking this action. (As preparation before meeting with a professional, review the classification rules in Appendix D.)

Summary of Payroll Expense

An excess of employees can sink any business. Keep reminding yourself of how you can control the cost of employees.

Do

☑ Be constantly aware of your total cost of an employee. For each class of employee, you should be able to come up with a percentage by which you should increase the actual pay rate in order to know what your total cost is.

☑ Frequently ask for bids from contractors for performing functions currently performed by employees, for sales, administrative, and production costs.

☑ Look for ways to increase the efficiency of employees.

Don't

☒ Offer employees higher wages in order to forgo benefits. It will make it almost impossible to offer benefits later when you need more employees.

☒ Lay off key employees that you may desperately need in several months. Instead, try to utilize them in lower-level tasks until business improves.

☒ Overlook how automation could reduce the need for manual processing and the number of employees needed.

Purchase of Equipment and Other Assets

In this technological age, it seems that, somewhere, someone makes a piece of equipment that will do almost everything you do in your business automatically or at least with less human effort. But the fact that it's automatic and may save worker-hours does not necessarily mean that this is the best use of your cash or your ability to borrow cash. There are some questions to be answered.

What is the skill level (and therefore the cost) of the employee whose time you are conserving? Obviously, a machine that saves manager time can be justified easier than a machine that saves time of a minimum-wage worker.

Does the proposed equipment really save worker time or is it more of a convenience? For instance, if your outgoing mail is all in regular No.10 envelopes weighing less than an ounce, it makes little sense to purchase a postage meter. It takes about the same amount of time to purchase stamps or recharge the postage meter either at the post office or online, so the meter would be only a convenience. However, if your daily mailing consists of different-sized packages and envelopes, your choice is either to take those to the post office daily and let the postal employee do the weighing and stamping, or purchase the equipment to do it in your office. In that case, it may be cost-effective to purchase or rent the equipment to use in-house.

What is the principal task for which you will use the equipment? Consider the purchase of a computer. If it will be used only for word processing, a less-expensive machine that does only word processing may be what you should consider. That is often true if you have other computers in your shop that can do e-mail, online research, accounting, and other business tasks.

Does having the latest equipment improve the appearance of your business and attract well-heeled customers? That is difficult to quantify, but here is an example:

A few years ago, when I had a copy machine without a document feeder, I needed to copy a 100-page document. As most all print shops at that time had copy machines with document feeders, I took my job to our local small-town print shop, expecting that I could have my document copied in a matter of five minutes and go on my way. I was, to say the least, surprised when I handed my document to the lady behind the counter and watched her as she picked up the lid on an old copy machine and manually placed each page on the glass, closed the lid, hit the copy button, removed the page, and repeated the process 99 more times. Did I go there later for some printing I needed? I didn't. I felt I would be at risk of the lady having to use the original Gutenberg press complete with handset type. That would mean that the job would take many hours for which I would be charged.

Moral: Appearance does matter. If you use outdated equipment, keep it in the back room. Please understand that I do not disapprove of using old or obsolete equipment, so long as it *efficiently* does the job for you, it works well, and you keep it hidden. On the contrary, I *recommend* using old equipment if it effectively conserves cash flow.

The Numbers That Justify Equipment Purchase

Many businesses attempt to make a decision about purchasing equipment based on a gut feeling. That can lead to erroneous decisions and misuse of one's cash flow. In order to make computations that can assist one in making a decision as to purchase of equipment, the following are needed:

+ Costs of the equipment.

+ Tax breaks that may be available for purchasing equipment.

+ Cost of the money (interest rate) needed to purchase the equipment.

+ How long the equipment will last until it becomes obsolete or inefficient or requires major rebuilding. (Accountants call this "useful life.")

+ Cost of labor replaced by the proposed equipment.

+ Cost of labor required to operate the proposed equipment.

Griselda owned and managed a glassware factory, which produced hand-blown glassware that was sold through her customer base of gift shops. Her factory employees consisted of six glass blowers, one glass wrapper, and one glass packer. Griselda received a visit from Pete, a salesman for an equipment manufacturer, who proposed that she purchase a robotic machine that would create glassware, complete with minor flaws that would be identical to hand-blown glass, wrap the glass products in bubble wrap, and pack them in shipping cartons. The installed cost of the equipment was $500,000.

Griselda wondered: If she bought the machine, laid off her eight existing employees, and hired an individual with experience in operating this equipment, would it be a wise investment? To attempt to answer that, she made the computation in Table 2-4 (shown on page 88), which determined that the payback period was 2.6 years. In other words, it would take 2.6 years to recover her investment of $500,000. Thereafter, she would be enjoying the savings from the machine.

There is one important item missing in this easy calculation, and that is the interest cost on the $500,000 invested. That's part of the picture, whether Griselda borrows the money or uses her own funds. When she uses her own funds, she gives up the interest that the money would earn if she invested outside of her business. (That's known as opportunity cost.) Griselda recognized this and computed the interest cost. As the machine is guaranteed to operate for five years with little maintenance, she assumes she can finance the purchase at 10 percent over five years using an installment loan. The total interest cost is then $137,411. Adding that to the cost of the machine results in a payback period of approximately 3.3 years. That gets closer to the five-year life of the machine and makes the investment questionable.

Perhaps you're an escapee from a large corporation, where you were often called upon to justify various expenditures, such as those for equipment. You probably thought that getting into a small business would relieve you of those burdens, but now you find you still have to make them if you are to keep your cash flow intact. I'm sorry about that, but it is a fact of business (any size) life.

	Annual Salary	Taxes & Benefits	Total Cost Per Employee	Cost of All Employees in Class
Present factory staff:				
6 glass blowers	$ 30,000	$ 4,500	$ 34,500	$ 207,000
1 wrapper	15,000	2,250	17,250	17,250
1 packer	15,000	2,250	17,250	17,250
Total annual factory payroll				241,500
Subtract:				
Operator for new machine	40,000	6,000	46,000	46,000
Reduction in labor cost if new machine purchased (annual savings)				$ 195,500
Proposed new equipment				
Automatic glass machine				$ 500,000

Payback period in years: divide cost of new machine by annual savings

$500,000 ÷ $195,500 = 2.6 years

Table 2-4: Purchase of automatic machine

Administrative Expense

Executives and business owners need to be on guard for two opposing concepts. First, there is a tendency of some managers to keep too few records and be sadly lacking if there is a threat of litigation or a visit from tax authorities. On the other hand, there is sometimes a tendency of administrative people toward empire-building—setting up a hierarchy of records that demands more employees, equipment, and training to maintain. Somewhere in between lies the optimum amount of effort and the required expenditure. Precise formulas don't exist to find that point, but there are actions an entrepreneur or executive can take.

Ask questions. Ask your administrative employees to explain why they follow certain procedures and encourage them to look for more efficient ways to accomplish a task. For instance, if an employee makes frequent visits to the office supply store, have him or her determine the delivery policy of the store and weigh any charges for delivery against the time and money it saves.

Insurance

You can look at insurance in one of two ways. First, you can consider that insurance should cover any conceivable loss you might have. The second is that insurance is for protection against losses from which you could not recover. That is, the risk is far larger than you want or can assume. As a ridiculous example of the first consideration, you could get insurance that would buy you a new pair of $10 sunglasses if you lost the pair you bought. Insurance such as in the second consideration would pay you nothing unless your loss exceeded some amount, such as $500 or $1,000. This, of course, refers to the deductible clause in most insurance policies.

When purchasing insurance, you need to decide how much loss you could absorb (pay out of your business pocket) without the cash flow being a major calamity. Try this approach: Put $1,000 in a separate bank account, under the seat cushion in your office chair, or in some other safe hiding spot. Then, when you purchase insurance, buy a policy with a $1,000 deductible. If you have a loss, simply reach under your seat cushion and cover that portion of the loss that the insurance company is not obligated to pay. Immediately thereafter, start putting the cash aside to cover the deductible for the next loss that may (although we hope not) incur.

There are some types of insurance you really don't need. For instance, you can buy insurance against losing your business records that are stored on the hard drive of your computer. However, if you follow a strict policy of backing up your critical files and storing at least one copy of a recent backup away from your business premises, you then have no need for that data insurance. (There are also services that will accept the backup data that you send them over the Internet and store it for you. However, make sure you find a reputable storage service.)

Take the time to discuss with your insurance agent or company what actions and policies you can take to reduce your premium. For instance, adequate sprinkler systems and/or fire extinguishers, with a routine of periodic inspection, can significantly lower fire insurance premiums.

If you are a professional and are susceptible to malpractice or other professional liability, you probably have insurance to cover potential claims. You are also aware, no doubt, of the expensive nature of these policies. Some professionals may take the higher risk of practicing without insurance (what is called "going bare"). This is a dangerous position; as an alternative to full protection, consider purchasing some coverage, so that at least your legal expenses in defending against a claim (successfully, we hope) will be covered.

Finally, in purchasing insurance, take time to obtain quotes from more than one company or agent. Even if you have been delighted with the service from your present insurer, it helps to know what others are charging. However, before switching insurance providers, check out their reputation for paying claims. This can be done best by checking with others in your field, such as at trade association meetings, chamber of commerce meetings, and similar opportunities (including those on golf courses).

Telephone Expense

The bottom line in discussing telephone expense is this: Do not blindly accept what your local telephone company tells you that you need in the way of telephone service and pay the resulting bills. Take the time to solicit quotations from other telephone equipment providers. Some of the equipment and software that they offer duplicate what the telephone company provides for less cost, and it now appears that some of this local service competition will be offered by major long-distance carriers. If you have several telephone lines, you very well may save significant cash. If you are a one-person, one-telephone, one-line business, then utilizing service provided by your local telephone company may be your best bet. At least, it will delay the purchase of equipment and give you time to look at alternatives.

Advertising Expense

Advertising can be a win-win use of cash flow, but unfortunately, it can also be a lose-lose proposition. If your advertising brings in enough sales so that your gross profit on the sales more than pays for the advertising, give yourself a gold star! If the advertising does not generate enough sales, you may have wasted your hard-earned cash. If you are a small retailer and advertise only in the local newspaper, you can get a reasonably good handle on the effectiveness of your advertising. However, if you also advertise on television and other media, how do you know which advertising brought in the cash and which advertising only spent the cash? If placing your ads is a last-minute, hurried response to frantic calls from the media salesperson, there's probably no way you can answer that question. However, if you plan your advertising, you should be able to tell which media is effective and thereby look like a genius.

So set up a plan, and in that plan, develop tracking codes so you can tell from where the business came. The suggestions that follow are, of course, not the only possibilities, but they may start your thinking juices doing their job.

Coupons in newspapers and magazines are the easiest things to code and track. On the coupon, tell the customer to bring it in to obtain a special discount or price. When you buy the advertising that contains the coupon, make sure the date and the name of the media appears on the coupon. (If you prefer, you can make up some code to put on the coupon instead of the actual information.) Collect all the coupons the customers bring in, sort them by date and media, and then you'll know which was the most effective advertising. The same coding of coupons can also work for direct mail, so you can tell which dates and which mailing lists bring the best results.

If you advertise on the Internet, include in each ad the code that the customer will have to repeat on an order blank or in a telephone call in order to receive the discount or special pricing.

When you advertise specific products on television, offer a special discount or a free item if people respond within a few minutes of the ad. That makes it easy to judge effectiveness of your advertising dollars.

If your sales are business-to-business, instruct your order takers to simply ask new customers which ad or referral caused them to call or come in. Most successful businesspeople understand why you ask and generally have no reason not to give you an honest answer.

In short, make sure that your advertising outflow generates a larger inflow.

Fees That Others Charge to Handle *Your* Money

Yes, there are lots of people out there who will do things for or to your money for a fee—banks, for instance. Banks used to make money just by loaning money at interest rates that were higherthan they paid to depositors or the Federal Reserve Banks. They still do, but they have developed plenty of other sources of income.

Service Charges

As you are most surely aware, all banks charge a service fee for maintaining a checking account for you or your business, which is effective if you keep less than a certain minimum balance in the account. It's preferable, generally but not always, to keep that minimum balance in the account. When is it not preferable? If the bank demands a high balance, that may or may not work out to be excessive interest.

For a commercial account, a bank charges an account maintenance fee of $15 per month, but it charges no fee if the account balance never drops to less than $3,000. Is that a good deal? Here's the calculation in Table 2-5:

Computation of Equivalent Interest of Bank's Account Maintenance Fee	
Annual fee = 12 × $15 monthly	$180.00
By keeping $3,000 in the account, you earn $180 in one year. That amounts to an interest rate of	
$180 ÷ $3,000 =	6.0%

Table 2-5

The 6-percent return is obviously a good deal in times when banks are paying 1 percent or less on money market and other cash accounts. By all means, keep the $3,000 (or whatever your bank's magic number is) in the account—that is, unless you can safely earn more than 6 percent elsewhere (as paying off a credit card that charges you 12 percent).

Charges for Sweep Accounts

Should you sign up for a sweep account (discussed in Chapter 1)? You can answer that with a calculation that is similar to the one in Table 2-5 for service charges. In this case, we'll suppose that the bank charges $25 per month for maintaining a sweep account and pays a 1-percent annual interest rate on the sweep account (the account where the excess cash is kept). The calculation you need to make is in Table 2-6 on page 95.

Computation of When a Sweep Account Makes Sense	
Annual fee = 12 × $20	$240.00
Balance needed in sweep account to earn $240 is computed by dividing annual fee by interest rate	
$240 ÷ .01 =	$24,000.00

Table 2-6

You will have to look through several months of bank statements, checking the balance the bank thinks you have rather than your checkbook balance. If the *average* (not the minimum) is mroe than $24,000, a sweep account may make sense. Note that when interest rates are higher, you can use the same formula to compute the lower balance that will be required to justify a sweep account.

Merchant Credit Card Processing

As covered in Chapter 1, offering your customers the ability to charge their purchases on a credit card can greatly enhance sales. However, as with most sales promotion ideas, there is a cost. Most banks have an arrangement in which they accept the card charges as a deposit and collect approximately the same amount from the bank that issued the credit card. The process by which banks interact in the credit card area is not too important for businesses, but the fees that the banks and credit card processing companies charge *is* important. Depending on your financial picture and other considerations, your bank may or may not provide merchant processing for you. However, there are many merchant processing companies that handle processing for businesses that banks have rejected. You'll probably find that there will be an amount (a percentage of the sale called the *discount*) deducted from each sales invoice. In addition, there will probably be a monthly charge for the service.

Be careful in selecting a merchant processor. There's a lot of spam in Internet e-mail that offers to set you up to handle credit cards, and the people operating those sites may or may not be trustworthy. Remember: These people will be handling your money. At least make sure they have a bricks-and-mortar address and telephone, and certainly you should check with the Better Business Bureau and/or Dun & Bradstreet.

Time to Analyze Your Whole Administrative System

If you're a larger enterprise with several administrative employees, a networked computer system, and an embryo bureaucracy, it may be time to study your whole administrative operation. This is not an area in which a business owner or general manager should invest a lot of time. Such a time investment could only result in breakdown of management of the rest of the business (sales and production), and that could result in more cash outflow.

It may, therefore, be time to call in an outside consultant. For starters, check with the accounting firm that currently prepares your tax returns and financial statements. They have a slight jump on other consultants, because they are somewhat familiar with your business. Also, recommendations from a good accountant should include procedures that result in better *internal control* (defined by the example that follows). You may find that your present accounting firm does not have the staff, time, or expertise to properly engage in systems and internal control design. If that's the case, you will have to go on a search for one that does. Look for one large enough to have a partner or manager dedicated to management consulting, but not so large that it has created its own bureaucracy— complete with higher fees.

You might limit your search to firms that are large enough to have partners or staff with the necessary expertise, yet small enough not to be caught up in their own bureaucracy and therefore have to charge more. And as you did when you hired your first accountant (I trust), ask for references and check with other entrepreneurs in the business community.

I mentioned "internal control." What is it, besides a term often used by accountants? Rather than use a convoluted definition, here's an example that should explain:

Jennifer owns the Useless Knickknack Variety Store, which she started just two years ago, and it has experienced phenomenal growth. Due to the growth, she hired George to be her bookkeeper and his sister Gretchen to be her administrative assistant. When Jennifer opened her store, she was conscientious about reconciling the totals in the cash register with the bank deposits. However as she ran out of time, she just deposited the money in the cash register and saved the cash register tape in a box labeled "to do when time permits." As usually happens, time never permitted matching the cash register records with the deposit receipts. When she hired George and Gretchen, she did not take the opportunity to reinstitute the reconciliation system. Now Gretchen just gathers whatever money is in the cash register and deposits it in the bank. When she returns from her trip to the bank, she gives the deposit receipt to George, who enters the total deposit in the accounting records as "sales."

Now we have a picture of very poor internal control. As there is no reconciliation between the cash register records and the bank deposits, Gretchen is free to not deposit all of the receipts. Furthermore, as the bookkeeper is her brother, he would be reluctant to even question whether Gretchen deposited all of funds that were receipts.

What would have been better internal control? Obviously, Jennifer should have set up a system in which the day's cash register receipts total was read by one person, who also entered those totals in the accounting records. Another unrelated person should collect the money from the cash registers, count it, make up the deposit ticket, and take it to the bank. By not checking with her accountant and thinking through the situation, Jennifer has left the door open for two related people, who are no relation to Jennifer, to skim off much of her funds.

This sort of *defalcation* (accountants' word for "theft") happens in many businesses. In fact, it is a major cause of excessive cash outflow and resulting business failures.

Reducing the Outflow of Tax Dollars

Taxes have always beset businesspeople. Caesar demanded his, the medieval monarchs demanded their share of the barons' profits, and today our local state and federal coffers seem to demand ever-increasing contributions. (Time and some money stand in seeking tax knowledge, and help can bring significant monetary reports.) As this is not a tax book, we won't get into details here, but what follows is a general discussion and lists of items that can help you focus your reading on tax rules and in seeking professional help.

Local Taxes

Cities, towns, and counties impose area taxes on businesses. They can consist of occupational licenses, property taxes, various fees and assessments, and, in a few cases, sales taxes and income taxes. Don't be complacent and just throw your money at every tax collector who shows up. You can read the city tax ordinances or you can visit City Hall and ask questions. Don't forget to visit the economic development office of your local government. People in that office are charged with attracting businesses to your locality, so they may be a good source of information about tax breaks that may be offered to certain businesses or certain locations.

State Taxes

Most states collect income taxes, sales taxes, and/or taxes on certain businesses such as gambling casinos. State income taxes on businesses are often modeled on the federal system or are simply a percentage levied on the profits of business computed in the federal tax return. Sales tax rules vary widely from state to state, as in fees such as those for professionals and skilled trades. If you are seeking a location for a new business or a branch of an existing business, time spent studying the state tax laws of possible locations can be rewarding. Fortunately, most states now post their tax code and regulations on their Internet sites, so tax information is more readily available. Still, a little guidance from a tax-oriented attorney or CPA is well worthwhile, if only to keep you out of trouble and away from penalties that can seriously impact your cash flow.

Federal Taxes

Federal income tax can be one of the largest factors in cash outflow. It is only those business managers who seek the best advice and plan carefully who can hope to diminish or eliminate this cash drain. There are some areas of income tax that deserve special attention by a business owner. What follows is a list of some of those areas with a brief description of each. Obviously, the details of this section fill many books (one of which I have written), so it is not a complete coverage of business taxes. But it is a list of items to consider and a checklist of what you may need to review with your tax advisor.

Choosing the Legal Form of Your Enterprise

There are several forms of conducting business, including sole proprietorship, partnership, limited liability company, S corporation, and C corporation.

A sole proprietorship exists any time in individual conducts a business owned solely by that individual. The painting contractor who operates a painting business by himself is a sole proprietor. If you ever mowed lawns for a few dollars as a kid, you were conducting a sole proprietorship. In other words, anyone who has not gone through the formalities of setting up a corporation, partnership, or a limited liability company is operating as a sole proprietorship. All profits (or losses) are added to the income on the income tax return of the sole proprietor.

A partnership is basically two or more individuals working together to operate a business. Profits or losses of the partnership are split between the partners, according to prior agreement, and each partner pays income tax on his or her share of the profits.

A limited liability company (LLC) can be thought of as they partnership in which the partners are not liable for the debts of the business beyond the amount of their investment in the business. Except in unusual circumstances, they are taxed as are partnerships—the members of the LLC report their share of the income on their individual income tax returns. (In an LLC, partners are known as "members" rather than as "partners.")

Corporations are viewed as a separate legal entity set up (chartered) by a state. They can be thought of as a separate person, apart from their owners (stockholders), entitled to some of the rights and obligations that are enjoyed by individuals. One of the obligations of a C corporation is to compute and pay its own income taxes, almost as a separate individual. (I say "almost" because tax rates applicable to C corporations are different from those for individuals.) S corporations differ from C corporations only in the manner in which they are taxed, as they are taxed similarly to a partnership or limited liability company. That is, the profits of an as corporation are split up between the stockholders and that income is included in their individual income tax returns. Also, there are limitations in the tax law as to who can be stockholders in an S corporation (individuals and some trusts) and the number of stockholders (75).

Because of differences in tax rates between corporations and individuals and other rules too numerous and complex to mention here, choosing the best business form for your situation can result in a significant lowering of tax liability, but the process is not cut and dried. There is no magic formula that will tell you that you definitely should choose one form over another. Also, as I write this, Congress is wrestling with the Presidents proposed tax reduction plan that might do away with (or reduce) the double taxation of dividends in C corporations, and that could significantly change the criteria for choosing to be a C or an S corporation. As the House and Senate are still billions of dollars apart on the tax reduction bill, including the details of a reduction or elimination of the double tax on dividends, it is impossible to suggest how to utilize these tax changes in planning your business form at this point. That means you should seek professional advice before selecting or changing to a specific business form.

Choosing the Best Accounting Method (Cash, Accrual, or Something Else)

Your choice of an accounting method determines when a business will pay tax on its profits. That is, will it pay tax today or a year or two years in the future?

Clem is in the snow removal business. On December 20, 2002, he plowed Dorothy's long driveway, for which he charged $100. He sent Dorothy an invoice for the job on December 28, and she sent him a check for $100 on January 10. Assuming Clem prepares his tax return on a calendar year basis, using the cash method, he would have reported the income in January of the new year, when Dorothy paid him. If he uses the accrual method, he would have reported the income in December 2002, the year when he made the sale. That would result in his paying the tax on the $100 fee one year ahead of when he would have paid it if he used the cash method.

If Clem plowed 100 driveways at $100 each during December and used the cash method rather than the accrual method, he would delay payment of the tax on $10,000 for one year. If the tax on that is $4,000, and Clem can turn 5 percent interest on his money, he has an additional $200 cash inflow.

So, everyone will use the cash method, right? Unfortunately, no. The IRS has rules about the types of businesses that may and may not use the cash method. So again, this is an area that deserves more study and/or professional advice. Suffice it to say here that if your gross annual sales are less than $1 million, you generally can use the cash method, no matter what business you are in. (Exception: Sales of items from inventory have to be matched with the cost of those items so that both the sales and costs are recorded in the same period.) At any rate, check it out. Keeping money in your pocket instead of the government's pocket is almost always a wise move, even if you have to give it up later. Note: Don't use procedures to keep the government's money when you shouldn't. That leads to the imposition of penalties, which are expensive and defeat the whole point of delaying payment.

The IRS will also accept some other specialized accounting methods. For instance, if you're in the construction business and have a contract that extends two or more years, there are special rules that allow you to report the income as a project progresses.

Inventory Valuation

This is another area that, with proper planning, will allow you to keep cash in your pocket and send it much later to the U. S. Treasury.

Ernie sells pencils on the street corner. Yesterday morning he purchased 100 pencils from the wholesaler for $.04 apiece ($4). He sold 70 pencils at $.10 apiece. His cash flow was sales of $7 minus the $4 he paid the wholesaler, for a $3 net cash inflow. However, his taxable profit is the $7 sale minus the cost of the 70 pencils ($2.80), or $4.20 profit.

Today, Ernie purchased another 100 pencils, but was unpleasantly surprised because the wholesale price had risen to $.06 a pencil. Ernie continued to sell the pencils at $.10 apiece, but sold only 30 pencils as the weather was rainy. Now Ernie has to compute his taxable profit on those 30 pencils. He has to decide whether the pencils he sold were the 30 left over from yesterday at the constant $.04 apiece or were they those 30 that he bought today at $.06 apiece! As Ernie, like the rest of us, wants to pay as little tax as possible, he elected to assume that the pencils he sold today came out of the lot that he purchased at $.06 apiece. In other words, he decided to use a system that says he sold the last pencils he bought first—or the last pencils were the first pencils out. Accountants call that the LIFO (Last-In, First-Out) system. That meant his profit was $1.20. If Ernie decided that he sold the pencils left over from yesterday, he would have been using the FIFO (First-In, First-Out) system, which meant his cost of the pencils sold was $.04 apiece. In that case, his profit would be $1.80.

Ernie, of course, must expand his sales many times over before he worries about income taxes. But the same principle applies to all companies with inventory, whether it's a Fortune 500 company or a mom-and-pop. So discuss inventory valuation with your tax advisor.

Note: If you are starting a business, telling the IRS what accounting and inventory system you selected is easy. Just use your selection for your first business tax return. If you make a wrong choice and want to change it in a later year, the process to request the IRS to approve your change is mind-boggling.

Depreciation

For centuries, accountants have used the concept of depreciation in computing the profit from a business. It works this way: If you buy a piece of equipment (a bulldozer, for instance) for $100,000, that action is an immediate cash outflow of $100,000. (Of course, there might be an offsetting cash inflow from the finance company.) The accountants' depreciation rules say that the cash outflow does not represent an immediate expense. That's because the bulldozer will last for five years, or at least you hope and expect it will last for five years. Therefore, one-fifth, or 20 percent, of the $100,000 cash outflow is an expense in each of those five years. This process of spreading the amount paid for the equipment over the life of the equipment and showing only a fraction of the amount paid as an expense in each of those years, is called depreciation.

Obviously if, from one transaction, you have a cash outflow of $100,000 and an expense of only $20,000, this depreciation calculation is a major factor in the difference between net cash flow and net income (profit). If depreciation were always this simple, this would be all we need to say about it, but as with everything in the tax area, it's been made complex over the years.

There's always a question that arises between the IRS and taxpayers as to how long equipment will last. If your bulldozer is used only for moving around loose sand, it may last well beyond five years. If you choose to move heavy boulders around, the life may be considerably shorter than five years. The IRS, of course, wants you to have a smaller depreciation tax deduction so it would like to insist that everything will last for 100 years; we taxpayers would like to say it should be 100 percent deduction in the year we buy the equipment. Congress has somewhat defused this contentious point by specifying that the IRS set up tables of lives of various classes of equipment. Your accountants can help you determine the IRS-approved life of your bulldozer.

About the same time that Congress took away our ability to argue with the IRS about depreciation, it provided a gift to small businesses. Current tax law allows businesses to treat the first $25,000 of equipment purchases as an expense and a deduction in computing the tax on business profits. Also, this gift is reduced if a small business purchases more than $200,000 of equipment. (The President's tax cut proposal, which the Congress is now debating, would raise this amount to $75,000 that could be deducted annually and the limit on equipment purchases, if a business is to be eligible for this deduction, would be raised to $325,000.)

This is not a definitive discussion of depreciation. It is here to explain a major difference between net cash flow and net income and to alert you to the tax effect—and, therefore, the cash flow effect—of properly planned equipment purchases. For instance, if you are planning to purchase $40,000 of equipment, buy half of that equipment in December and the other half the following January. That will put $20,000 of immediate tax deduction into each year. As always, you should involve your tax professional in this planning.

Hire Contractors
Rather Than Employees

As mentioned in Chapter 1, there is considerable expense in hiring employees beyond the wage paid to the employee, such as payroll taxes. The rates and computations are covered in Chapter 1, but covered here is the extreme importance that these taxes on the employer and those taxes withheld from the employees be remitted on time to the IRS and two-year state tax authority, assuming your state imposes income taxes.

Federal penalties look this way: If withheld employee taxes are not paid according to an IRS schedule, the penalty rate ranges from 2 percent to 15 percent of the amount that should have been paid, depending on how long it is until it is paid. There is also a penalty for failing to file the related tax forms: 5 percent tax per month up to a total of 25 percent. The IRS also charges interest and there may be additional penalties in certain cases. The bottom line is to protect your cash flow by filing the forms and paying payroll taxes on time. If you do not have a conscientious bookkeeper on your staff, you would be well advised to utilize an outside service.

You can avoid this payroll hassle if you utilize independent contractors to perform the duties that employees would otherwise perform. For instance, if you are a construction contractor building frame houses, you can hire carpenters and put them on your payroll and have payroll headaches. Alternatively, you could hire a framing contractor who, in turn, pays the actual carpenters and has to contend with the payroll headaches. But—and this is important—you cannot turn your administrative assistant into an independent contractor, because the IRS rules would prohibit this. If you decide to utilize contractors instead of employees, tread carefully and get advice from a tax-oriented attorney or CPA. To help you save some time (and fees) with a professional, the relevant IRS rules are reprinted in Appendix D. Note that if you classify someone as a contractor when the IRS classifies the individual as an employee, you will have seriously jeopardized your cash flow. You'll probably incur professional expenses in contesting the IRS's decision and, if you lose, there will be serious penalties and employment taxes to pay.

Travel, Meals, and Entertainment Expense

This is another area with complex tax rules, which are best explained in books that concentrate on tax questions. However, if you travel on business or have employees who travel (and you pay the expenses), you know how fast the dollars can disappear when one is out of town. Believe it or not, Uncle Sam will pay part of those travel and entertainment expenses by allowing you to deduct at least a portion of them on your income tax return.

You can significantly reduce your cash outflow in this area if you learn the rules. Perhaps the most important rule is to keep a contemporaneous log of your travel and entertainment activities. Yes, it's a real burden on managers with other important concerns, but if you don't keep those records an IRS examiner can disallow your travel and entertainment deductions, assess penalties and interest, and make not only your cash flow, but also your whole life, miserable.

Other Taxes

Although I have dwelt at some length on federal income taxes, that is not to say there are not other federal taxes that impact cash flow. Among these are import duties and taxes on certain products, such as alcohol and tobacco. If you are in an industry that is subject to these types of taxes, you should be able to obtain informative help from your trade association or professionals who specialize in your type of business.

As mentioned before, state taxes are also significant. Be sure you are in compliance with state tax rules and avoid penalties that can be imposed by state tax regulators.

CHAPTER 3

What to Do With Excess Cash

Someday, if you follow the advice in this and other books, listen to your accounting, tax, and legal professionals, do the right things, and have some luck, you should find yourself or your business with much more cash than you need. Yes, Virginia, that does happen. According to the *Wall Street Journal*, at the end of 2002, Microsoft held a cash hoard of $40 billion, Cisco had cash in the amount of $21 billion, and Intel, Dell Computer, and Oracle also hold billions in cash balances.[1] And they are all in the tech industry, which is supposed to be struggling. Maybe someday it will be you—rather than Bill Gates—who is world-famous for your billions.

When you find yourself no longer sweating payroll days and able to afford some decent artwork and drapes for your office, what will you to do with the excess cash? One possibility is to splurge on new buildings and fancy equipment that you always wanted to own but couldn't have because such acquisitions didn't pass the analysis that we covered in Chapter 2.

Another possibility is to go on a buying spree that consists of purchasing other companies. You could grow your company to the point that your stock is listed on the New York Stock Exchange or the NASDAQ and use your stock to swallow companies far larger than yours, just as America Online swallowed Time-Warner.

But on the way to that game with the big boys, there are some less expensive ways to efficiently use extra cash. Let's consider some of them.

Take Care of the Owners (Stockholders) of Your Business

You and probably some other individuals in your top management put in long, sweaty hours to build the business that now has a cash surplus. Also, there may have been investors in your business who took a large risk in providing the funding to get you started. Now may be the time to dole out a few rewards. (For this discussion, we'll assume your business is incorporated. If you have adopted the mantle of a limited liability company, please see the comments at the end of this section.)

Pay Dividends to Stockholders

While this is the simplest manner by which to pull the accumulated profits of a C corporation out of it, it has a large downside, which is the double taxation of dividends that was covered in Chapter 2. While you can avoid this problem by becoming an S corporation, not all business ventures can fit the requirements to be an S corporation. So, if your business is a C corporation, and unless the Congress changes that two-tiered tax system, you will want to find other ways to take profit out of the corporation. One popular way is through salaries, discussed next.

Pay Higher Salaries to Stockholders and Employees

Paying yourself (and other employees who are also stockholders) a higher salary is one way to extract money from your corporation, but there are some tax hurdles to jump in this area, particularly as to the reasonableness of the salary. If the IRS thinks your salary is too high for the size and nature of your business, it will reclassify some of your salary to dividends, and that means you will suffer the double taxation—if the law doesn't change.) What salary level for a stockholder/employee is too high? There are no firm rules. Generally, the IRS will look at what level is common in your geographical area, in your industry, and for your size of business. Incorrect estimation of what the IRS will accept can be disastrous on your cash flow, so again this calls for professional help.

There is also an equity problem with salaries. If some stockholders are employees of the corporation and others are not, it is almost impossible to treat all stockholders equitably via salaries. Unfortunately, it is illegal to pay some stockholders salaries while others receive dividends, as dividends have to be paid equally on all shares of stock.

Cause the Corporation to Invest the Excess Cash

C Corporations can follow this scenario: When your earnings become so large that you cannot withdraw them from the corporation by paying higher salaries (because the IRS would call them unreasonable) you can apply the extra cash towards making the corporation more valuable. In other words, pursue an active expansion program that will eventually increase the profits of the corporation and thereby the value of your stock in the corporation. You can have a goal of eventually selling your enterprise, which means that your accumulated earnings will flow to you as proceeds of a sale of the business, and (if properly structured) reduce the tax rate on the proceeds to lower capital gain rates.

How you expand the corporation's business can take several forms: Increase advertising and other sales efforts, buy other businesses, start other businesses from scratch, and whatever appears to increase your success. Caution: Do not embark on a program of merely making passive investments in the stock market with corporate funds, as long-term capital gain rates do not apply to corporate profits from stock investments. (There are some exceptions, such as mutual funds and real estate investment trusts, but a company engaged in active business such as manufacturing, distribution, and services cannot qualify for these classifications.)

Buy Back Your Stock

No, we are not yet talking about your being listed on the stock exchange and simply buying your stock up through a broker. We are talking about people such as your Uncle Leo, who helped you get started in your embryo enterprise. At that time, Uncle Leo was doing well in his small chain of steakhouses and advanced $300,000 for 30 percent of the common stock in your small, new corporation. Now, Uncle Leo is 65, has sold his restaurants, and has the means to live comfortably but not enough to buy the yacht that would take him and your aunt to the Virgin Islands and Europe. So it is time for you to return the favor to Uncle Leo. Besides, Uncle Leo's son and daughter (your cousins) are somewhat spoiled and unsuccessful know-it-alls. That hardly equates to the kind of people you would like to have as partners in your successful operation. So, at the same time you do Uncle Leo a favor, you will also be doing yourself a favor by making sure that the stock in your corporation, owned by Uncle Leo at present, will not one day end up in the hands of your less-than-desirable cousins. Those are two very good reasons to spend part of that cash to buy back Uncle Leo's stock in the corporation—for a figure that reflects the growth of net worth in your business.

Be sure you obtain advice from a knowledgeable tax professional when you buy out a stockholder. There are tax traps involved in this type of transaction.

Pay Dividends to the Stockholder (You)

This may or may not be a good policy, depending on how the tax laws change between now and the time when you have the extra cash available. At present, corporate earnings are taxed twice—once to the corporation and the second time to the stockholder when dividends are paid. If this two-tier taxation is not changed, you will want to find other ways to take money out of your corporation. (This applies if you are a regular or C-type corporation. S corporations operate under different rules that allow for only one-time taxation of earnings, but they have other tax challenges.)

If the tax code discourages paying dividends, you will have to look into other means of extracting the cash from your corporation. Paying yourself a higher salary is one way, but there are some tax hurdles to jump in this area, particularly with regard to the reasonableness of the salary.

If You Do Business as a Limited Liability Company (LLC)

If your business form is an LLC, you do not have the challenges associated with the double taxation of dividends, nor do you have certain limitations that are imposed on S corporations. Generally, if an LLC has the cash in the bank, it can choose to distribute most of it, if not all, to its members without additional tax. However, when a member of an LLC sells his or her interest in the LLC, there are some tax snares—the avoidance of which will require the help of a tax professional. (This comment assumes your LLC has elected to be taxed as a partnership, as do most LLCs.)

Attract the Best Employees

If your business is to continue to grow, you need to hire those with the best talent, skills, and training. People who are in demand look for not only cash compensation, but medical insurance, a retirement plan, and other benefits, including the view from their office window.

Refine Your Employee Benefit Plans (Pension, 401(k), Medical, etc.)

For most entrepreneurs, benefit plans have three goals:

+ The first is to enable the entrepreneur to transfer substantial cash from the corporation to his or her personal funds while avoiding a tax bite.

+ The second is to enable the corporation to attract people with superior talent and dedication to its employee ranks.

+ The benefit plans should provide the most bang for the buck—the greatest benefits for the lowest cash outflow.

As one of the largest outflow items is the income tax bill, it behooves you to make sure your employee benefit plans are carefully constructed around the tax rules. To accomplish that, the goal in setting up an employee benefit plan is for the cost of the plan to be deductible by the employer and not taxable to the employee. The cost of medical insurance is a good example of a benefit that fits this profile.

John works for Mary. Mary has installed a medical insurance plan for all employees, and John's coverage costs $400 per month, which Mary pays. That is, the $400 is part of John's compensation. However, because it is a qualified medical plan, Mary can deduct the $400 cost of the insurance, but the $400 is not taxable income to John.

A retirement plan, such as a pension plan or a 401(k), works in a similar manner to the medical plan, but there is some tax for the employee to pay in the future, when he or she retires and withdraws the pension or savings from the plan. The theory is that the employee will be in a lower tax bracket and will therefore pay little or no tax on those benefits.

Perhaps you have had no retirement plan during your initial entrepreneurship years or you had a Simplified Employee Pension (SEP) plan. In either event, now that you can afford it, it is time to engage a professional who specializes in retirement plan installation. A more sophisticated plan may generate more tax advantages to you—the owner of the business.

Stock Options Issued to Employees Save Cash

Issuing incentive stock options to your employees is a great way to reduce your cash outflow. Although there is current agitation to require corporations to list the value of stock options as a compensation expense on their financial statements, it's an expense for which the corporation writes no checks. Although it is not a tax deduction for the corporation, granting the option generates no cash outflow. However, it does generate cash inflow when the employee exercises the option, although that event probably will be some years in the future. Note that these stock options have little value to the employee unless the stock in your corporation is publicly traded or soon will be publicly held. Also, if specific rules are properly followed, the income to the employee when the stock is sold is considered capital gain.

Using Excess Cash to Accelerate the Growth of Your Business

If your bills are being paid on time and you have a cash hoard (no matter what size), you may be tempted to spend some of it to increase sales. Certainly, increased sales should be the goal of every enterprise, provided the increase in sales generates more gross profit than the cost of making the sale. (Gross profit, as used here, means the sale minus the cost of the merchandise and minus other direct costs, such as the salesperson's time, delivery costs, and so on.)

> Tina was in the backyard party tent business. She sold these tents in upper-middle-class neighborhoods for $500 each. They cost $300 each, the order fulfillment firm charged her $20 for processing the order, and she contracted Clem to erect the tent in the backyard of the customers at $100 for each tent. That left her just $80 gross profit. Tina had been making phone calls and knocking on doors to sell the tents, but now Shirley offered to do the sales work for a $90 commission on each tent. Obviously, Tina could not afford to pay that commission, for it would generate a negative cash flow of $10 on each tent. So, spending that extra commission money to increase sales would be a foolhardy decision.

Building up the Inventory

If you're in the wholesale or retail business, you have no doubt felt pain when you didn't have an item a customer was ready and willing to buy. Now, you think, you can stock everything that customer could possibly need or want to. Before you do, review the inventory sections of Chapter 2. Analyze the true cost of your inventory, including interest on the investment, storage space, insurance, stock room employees, and the possibility that the inventory will spoil or become obsolete.

Probably you'll find that it doesn't pay to stock slow-moving items. Sam Walton must've come to that decision early on in his original store. Even today, if an item doesn't turn over fairly fast, you won't find it at Wal-Mart.

About the only justification for stocking slow-moving items is when they act similarly to a loss leader. That is, they attract customers into an enterprise where, we hope, they will also buy more profitable items or services. For instance, assume that gold plated hinges for bedroom doors have become the rage, so you stock them in your hardware store. Obviously, you will then have to stock various lengths of gold-plated screws to match the hinges. Then, as it becomes known that you stock odd fasteners such as gold screws, new customers who need unusual (and slow-moving) nuts, bolts, and screws will show up in your store. You have created a traffic-builder. (This is an example of how a local hardware store can compete with the big-box stores, where the nut, bolt, and screw buyer can fail to coordinate with the hinge buyer and leave the sales clerk with the quandary of how to sell the gold hinges without the matching screws.)

Acquiring More Equipment and Other Fixed Assets

The same advice as for building up inventory applies here. Review the payback computation in Chapter 2. If you so choose, you could also compute the internal rate of return for the equipment. That's not too hard to do if you're mathematically inclined and have a financial calculator, or if you are familiar with the functions available in a good spreadsheet software program.

There is, however, a distinction between the days when you were strapped for cash and these days when you have extra funds. In the payback for its computations, if you must borrow the funds, the interest rate in your computation should be what a lender will charge you. When you make the computation now, the interest rate in the computation should be what you can earn if you invest the same money in a reasonably safe investment.

If you simply must have that heavy-duty diesel truck with the dual rear wheels to deliver your factory's output of feather pillows, realize that you are buying a toy and that its cost should come out of your personal toy budget, not out of your business equipment budget.

Acquiring Other Companies

Acquisition was a game the big boys played constantly during the 1990s, with the expectation that some kind of synergy would bring greater efficiencies and higher profits when two companies joined together. Some of these acquisitions actually helped the acquiring company, but it appears that, in most cases, both parties to the acquisition only managed to survive and do almost as well as they might have done if they were still separate. Others, such as Tyco, bought every enterprise in sight, but found there was little or no resulting synergy. The mergers apparently did not result in efficiencies, so they tried to put a happy face on this situation by turning their accounting into a work of fiction. The rest of these acquisition-bent companies are now barely surviving, whereas others already have or soon will go the bankruptcy route.

If you are thinking of using your cash flow to buy another company, lay out a careful business plan just as you did, or should have done, before you opened your doors for business. In other words, watch every dollar just as you did back then. If you don't, you may find that the enterprise you purchased had a negative cash flow (carefully hidden from you) that may suck all of the positive cash flow out of your present business and leave you with the problem of too little rather than too much cash.

Sometimes the opportunity to acquire another business comes early in the history of a new enterprise. The same caveat of looking ahead and controlling the "urge to merge" that applies to large corporations also applies to a small business.

Sigmund owned a swimming pool maintenance company. This is obviously a very seasonal business, as pool openings start in the middle of April and pool closings end in late October. A handful of customers do have indoor pools, and that is enough to keep Sigmund busy during the winter, but every fall he is forced to lay off his three employees and hope they can find some work during the winter and will be available to work for him again in the spring. Some years the same employees do come back, but in other years Sigmund has to train new employees.

After five years of business, Sigmund had built up some cash reserves when he heard about Ronald. It seems that Ronald owned a snow-removal business, but he was in his late 60s and anxious to sell and retire. Sigmund met with Ronald, and they discussed a price and schedule of payments that Ronald would accept. Sigmund did not make a firm offer, but went home to consider this perceived opportunity.

Sigmund's first impulse was to add the income from the pool business and the snow-removal business together and dwell on what the total profits would be. However, he decided to first analyze what advantages and disadvantages would result from this business acquisition, so he came up with some questions that needed to be answered. The more important ones were:

◇ Did the business's seasons mesh, or would there still be dead times between the seasons in the spring and fall?

◇ Would the same people who performed pool installations and maintenance be capable of operating snow-removal equipment?

◇ Was there any existing equipment that would be useful in both businesses?

◇ Would the combination justify the purchase of any equipment that could be used in both businesses?

◇ What was Ronald's cash flow from this business? Was it sufficient to keep Sigmund's employees busy during the winter?

◇ What was the growth potential in terms of new customers?

◇ Were there any income tax ramifications?

Sigmund answered the questions, to himself, this way:

◇ Yes, there would be short dead times between the seasons. Sigmund would still have to lay off employees in the spring and fall, but it would be a temporary layoff for only two or three weeks. That should be more attractive to the employees than the former layoff period of several months, so they would probably stick around and wait for the busy season. That is, the acquisition should result in the employees staying with Sigmund's business for several years, which would reduce his time and effort spent in finding and training new employees.

◇ Sigmund has always made a point to hire employees who can handle the equipment needed to install a pool, such as a backhoe. Anyone who can operate a backhoe should have little problem with snow-removal equipment.

◇ As to the question of existing equipment, Sigmund wasn't sure. It could be that there was a plow attachment available for the backhoe that he owned, but he would have to check on that the next day.

◇ As for determination of Ronald's cash flow and the question of tax implications, Sigmund decided that it would be worthwhile to engage his accountant to look through Ronald's books and answer the tax question.

Although Sigmund could answer some of these questions off the top of his head, others would require careful analysis and computation. Sigmund was wise to decide to involve his accountant, particularly in the area of determining Ronald's cash flow from the snow-removal business. One of the difficulties in buying a small business is the determination as to whether the bookkeeping is complete and accurate. Generally, in the area of small businesses, a full-blown audit by a CPA firm is far too expensive to be cost-effective. However, as Sigmund's accountant ferrets through Ronald's books, he or she may (or may not) find inconsistencies that indicate that the books are not the whole picture of the business. That's an added benefit of having an accountant assist in determining whether or not the purchase of an additional business makes sense.

The message from this example of Sigmund is that successful acquisition of another business requires much homework. In essence, when you acquire another business, you are significantly changing the picture of your existing business by this addition. Therefore, the analysis is essentially the creation of a new business plan for the expanded enterprise consisting of both the existing and the purchased business. As for what should be in that business plan, see Chapter 4.

Merging Into a Larger Enterprise

A discussion about the acquisition of other businesses would not seem complete without a mention of a merger of your business into a larger business. In essence, such a merger is the sale of your business with the expectation that you and your executive staff will have commensurate duties, responsibilities, and compensation in the merged entity.

As for the cash flow, if you are paid cash for your ownership interest in your present business, the positive cash flow is a given. If you are paid for your company by stock in the company into which you are merging, your cash flow may become an unknown. Be careful of the constraints that may come with the stock, such as not being able to sell it for some period of time. That constraint assumes you can sell it, at some time, because the purchasing corporation is publicly traded. If its stock is not publicly traded, you need to exercise a great deal of due diligence before merging. At the very least, you need a contract that guarantees you and your key executives compensation that continues for several years, regardless of whether you managed to fit into the management of the acquiring corporation.

The business press frequently has news of mergers of large corporations that were unsuccessful in preserving the managements of both companies. Mergers of privately held companies are no different. They are risky and should not be undertaken without a contract that guarantees you will not be left out in the financial cold. By all means, engage a lawyer with merger and acquisition experience.

CHAPTER 4

Predicting and Planning Cash Flow

Because you've read this far, you probably are well on your way to controlling your cash flow. You've tightened up on accounts receivable, you're taking advantage of extended terms from your suppliers, and you're following the rest of the advice in this book. Will the advice work? Will it really keep you in business, turn your business into a cash machine, and provide you with the means to enjoy life? If you have the good fortune to have a crystal ball that foretells the future, you have but to glance into it to answer those questions. But believe it or not, there are a few lucky individuals who don't need a crystal ball.

Veronica's Uncle Vinny owned and operated a broom manufacturing plant that produced an outstanding, clean-sweeping product creatively called "Vinny's Brooms." Not only did Vinny use exceptional straw in the millions of brooms he produced, but he was fussy about the broomsticks. Lately, he had been receiving sticks made out of inferior lumber, complete with knot-holes and other blemishes. Vinny considered expanding into the broomstick manufacturing business, but decided against it, as it would entail additional management and production staff, manufacturing facilities, and other headaches he didn't want. So he offered to set Veronica up in the broomstick manufacturing business and guaranteed that she would sell 5 million broomsticks to him every year. In addition, he guaranteed that he would adjust the price he paid her for each broomstick, depending on variations in the wholesale price of lumber. In other words, Veronica had the equivalent of a crystal ball; she knew what her sales were going to be and what her profit margin was going to be.

If you're like the rest of us—no crystal ball and no Uncle Vinny—the best you'll be able to do is forecast and project[1] some numbers, which can give you some idea of where you're going, financially. The benefits of having some handle on the future are many. It can help plan the hiring or layoff of personnel. It can enable you to plan your purchasing of the product or material so you don't end up with excess that has to be sold at a loss or a shortage that cuts you out of some sales. And most importantly, it can forecast that time when your cash flow may dry up. If you see such an event coming in the future, you would have the opportunity to arrange for more funds well before you need them, and well before the lender (your banker) is aware that you may be running into cash flow problems. In other words, if you see tight times coming, you can arrange a line of credit now rather than later, when it may be difficult to do. Please do not enter a business as do some entrepreneurs—with the same attitude with which they would approach a roulette table in Vegas: "We'll give a try, and if it works, great." If it doesn't work, they go about reciting the hackneyed phrase "nothing ventured, nothing gained." But one of the great things about a business venture is that, unlike a gambling casino, you can change the odds to be substantially in your favor.

Gathering Information for Your Cash Flow Plan

If the odds are to be in your favor, you need to have hard facts and numbers from which to build a plan. If you have been in business for at least two or three years, hard facts and numbers exist in your financial records. If your sales volume in each of the last three years was $1 million, it is unrealistic (except in rare instances) to expect your sales this year to be $10 million. Using those historical facts, and modifying them for changing circumstances, you can project what is likely to happen in the coming months and year. However, taking last year's figures or the average of the last two or three years, increasing them by 10 percent, and considering *that* your plan may be woefully inadequate. Consider these questions and the answers that you need to supply. Breaking down your operation into several ingredients this way should enable you to do a better job of financial forecasting.

+ What will sales volume be? If it will increase or decrease, why?

+ Will you be able to raise prices to cover increases in your costs?

+ What will be the wholesale cost of your merchandise or the cost of materials for production as a percentage of your sales?

+ Will wage rates remain static, or will you have to increase your payroll costs and the costs of employee benefits?

+ Will rent and other overhead costs of production increase?

+ Will general and administrative expenses rise?

If you are starting a business, or at least thinking about it, your task is more daunting. Some of your challenges can best be listed as questions that need answers. For example, do you have answers for these questions?

✦ Who will be your customers? Where are they currently buying the product or service you propose to furnish? What would make them change from their current vendor to your business?

✦ If you attract business by selling at a lower price, will you still be able to generate a profit?

✦ Is your proposed location suitable for your proposed type of business?

✦ What sort of advertising and other marketing will you conduct?

✦ What skill level will you demand from your employees? Will you be able to afford the going rate in your area?

Following are some possible actions and ideas to help you answer these questions and thereby create a meaningful plan that will ensure positive cash flow.

Sales Volume

Predicting sales volume is perhaps the most difficult aspect of this determination of probable future. That's because it's the area over which you have the least control. You certainly can do things to influence it, such as increasing your advertising, increasing your sales staff, helping your dealers to increase customer volume (such as through co-op advertising), and implementing other promotions. Whatever you do, *don't just guess*.

Start by being aware of general economic conditions, both in the country and in your market area. At least read the business section of your local newspaper and extend that to business magazines or business newspapers such as the *Wall Street Journal.*

Join and be active in your trade association. This is a source of information and possibly the only route to exchanging information with competitors without running afoul of restraint-of-trade laws. (Trade associations generally have rules, which have to be followed, keeping you on the right side of the law.) If you don't know if there is a trade association, check with your library see if it has a copy of *Gale's Directory of Associations.* It is reported to be out of print, but it may still be helpful. As an alternative, do research on the Internet by typing the name of your industry and the word *association* into a search engine window.

Along with activity in your trade association, join your local chamber of commerce and be active there. At least it will give you exposure with other entrepreneurs and a feel for general business in your area. At best it will give you contact with people who may become your customers.

Survey your market area. If you are a manufacturer or wholesaler, ask your customers how much they may be buying from you in the next quarter or the next year. If you are a retailer, drive around and otherwise be aware of demographic changes in your market area. (Are there new housing developments? Has highway construction changed traffic flow? Do you have new competitors in the area? Has an old competitor gone out of business?) If you are in a service business where consumers are your customers, many of the same questions apply to you as to retailers. If your service is to businesses, then you, like wholesalers or manufacturers, can ask your customers.

The hard part is reducing the facts you have found to numbers in your plan, but sometimes it can be done almost accurately. For instance, you may find that there are 300 new homes in your market area. They have been added to the 3,000 homes existing a year ago. That may justify an expectation of a 10-percent gain in sales, or possibly more, inasmuch as these new residents have yet to build a loyalty to any particular vendor of your product or service.

Pricing Policy

Unless your customers are in the high-end luxury market, lower prices generally attract more business. But a decision to lower prices runs up against the irrefutable economic law: Your prices must be high enough to cover your costs or you will spiral into the maelstrom of negative cash flow. More cash flow volume does not do you a bit of good unless some of that cash flow sticks to you. But you can determine an acceptable pricing level with some calculations. Later in this chapter we cover the forecasting of cash flow by computations, and those same computations can tell if the difference between sale price and cost price is adequate.

Costs of Merchandise or the Manufacturing of Merchandise

If you're operating a retail or wholesale business, general conversation with your suppliers should give you some indication of whether price increases are imminent. Whatever you find out from existing suppliers, don't overlook opportunities for better prices from competing sources. If you're manufacturing a product, the same advice about suppliers holds true and, in addition, applies to the cost of labor. If you are just opening a business, check with your state labor authority about prevailing wage rates for a given skill in your location.

Overhead and Other Costs

Certain expenses, such as rent, are fairly predictable. For instance, rent may be determined by a lease that locks in that expense, unless you have a lease that calls for a basic rate and percentage of sales, as is common in mall retail locations. Other expenses, such as employee benefits, travel and entertainment, telephone service, and computer maintenance and upgrades, can get out of hand quickly, so they demand management's attention. Again, if you're starting a business, spend some time on the phone or the Internet, and get all the prices and facts you can.

Putting the Cash Flow Numbers Together

Now that you have obtained the best numbers you can for the factors that determine cash flow (and profits), the numbers need to be put together in a format that will make sense out of them. As you probably realize, the numbers you have relate more to determining net income, or profit, than to determining cash flow. For instance, a jeweler may have a good customer to whom she extends credit and to whom she sells a $5,000 brooch in December, receiving the check from the customer in January. The sale is in December when the jewelry goes from her hand to the customer's hand, but the cash flow doesn't happen for a month.[2] That's the reason we start this computation by computing net income first. (That's sort of a halfhearted explanation, but a wholehearted explanation would fill another book.)

Floyd Floatem and Sidney Sinkem are planning to open a boat sales and repair business on January 1 of next year in a New England coastal town. They have accomplished a reasonably good job of doing their homework in that they do know how many boats are within 25 miles of their location, the size of the boats, the demographics of the area (income, age, etc.), and the number, capabilities, and skill of existing competitors. Considering all of the known factors, they have put together an income statement for their first year in business, displayed in Table 4–1 on page 135.

Happily, this shows a net income of $134,000 on sales of $1,255,000, and that is after paying corporate income tax of about $58,000.[3] The net income is computed after payment of basic salaries to Floyd and Sidney, with the result—both of them were sure—that they would be very successful. However, they wisely recognized that in order to sell boats, one must have some boats on hand—in inventory. Although they were each planning to invest $50,000 in this start-up business, they assumed they would need additional cash in order to purchase inventory equipment and other essentials. Therefore, they applied to the bank for a loan and thereby started on the convoluted course of paperwork and conferences that would secure approval of both the Small Business Administration and the bank. The size of the requested loan ($200,000) was determined by a seat-of-the-pants guess.

The first bit of paperwork requested by the loan officer was a breakdown of the first-year sales and expenses month by month rather than just the year's

Floatem & Sinkem Sales & Repair
Forecast of Income Statement
End of First Year

Sales:

Boat sales	$ 510,000	
Accessories and parts sales	265,000	
Repairs & accessory installation	480,000	
Total Sales		$ 1,255,000

Cost of sales:

Boats	382,500	
Parts & accessories	159,000	
Direct labor	161,700	
Sales commission	62,750	
Total cost of sales		765,950
Gross profit		489,050

General & administrative expenses:

Executive & admin. salaries	132,000	
Advertising	36,000	
Rent	36,000	
Utilities	6,000	
General insurance	4,800	
Legal and accounting fees	10,000	
Telephone & Internet expense	6,000	
Office supplies	1,500	
Vehicle expenses	7,200	
Travel expenses	2,000	
Licenses and fees	5,500	
Depreciation	31,000	
Total general & admin. exp.		278,000
Net operating income (loss)		211,050
Other expense, interest		18,539
Net income before tax		192,511
Federal income tax		58,329
Net income after tax		$ 134,182

Table 4-1: F & S Income Statement

total that Floyd and Sidney had computed. That took a few hours of evenings and weekends to create. The loan officer had suggested that it would not be proper to just divide the year's total by 12, considering that the boat business in that part of the country was very seasonal. That is, he would expect to see much higher sales in late winter and early spring than in late summer and fall, at the end of the boating season.

Nevertheless, Floyd and Sidney developed the monthly income statement that is shown in Table 4-2 on pages 138 and 139. The loss in the first month is to be expected in a new business. Indeed, many businesses suffer losses for many months or years.

When the banker looked at this monthly income statement, he was concerned that what had been profits actually turned into losses in the late fall. So his question was this: Would the proceeds of the loan be sufficient to see the business through the lean period in the fall? To answer that, he asked the entrepreneurs to compute a cash flow statement for the first year on a month-by-month basis. When Floyd and Sidney attempted to put this document together, they came to realize that they were boat people, not accountants. So they hired an accountant and, in exchange for a fee, received the document in Table 4-3 on pages 140 and 141.

We'll interrupt this story in order to take a closer look at Tables 4-2 and 4-3. Obviously, in the cash flow statement, cash inflows do not equate to sales. In January, of course, the cash inflow includes the investment by the owners and the proceeds of the bank loan. Although total sales were $40,000, the cash flow statement shows cash from sales of only $27,500. The reason for this discrepancy is that the owners anticipate they will collect only half of the current repair billing in the current month. That's because certain customers will not have paid for repairs by the end of the month. For instance, Floyd and Sidney expect to contract with insurance companies to repair boats of their customers that suffer damage, and insurance companies do take some time to generate checks.

When Floatem & Sinkem repair a boat for an individual customer, the customer is billed for the repair when it is completed. The boat is not released to the customer until the bill is paid. Customers who live from payday to payday tend not to pick up their boat and pay the bill until after a payday or so. That means the work product has been billed, but the boat remains at Floatem & Sinkem until the bill is paid. In other words, it is an account receivable until the boat is picked up. For those reasons, Floyd and Sidney estimate that only 50 percent of a month's repair billing will be paid in that month, 35 percent will be paid in the month following, and the final 15 percent will be paid in the third month after the work is completed. Accordingly, receipts shown as cash inflows lag sales by weeks.

For boat sales, the sales figure is the same as the cash inflow figure. That's because the title to a boat is not transferred to the customer until the day the customer shows up with certified checks or a check from a bank or finance company.

Under *cash outflows* in the January column, the first item is $100,000 to purchase boats. Yet, on the income statement, there is a cost of boat sales of only $11,250 for one boat sold that month (see Table 4-2). That is, the wholesale price paid for a boat does not become a cost to be deducted from sales until the boat is sold. Where does the other $88,750 of boat purchases show up? It's in the inventory of boats on January 31.

FLOATEM & SINKEM BOAT SALES & REPAIR — Forecast of Monthly Income Statement — First Year (Part I)

	JAN	FEB	MAR	APR	MAY	JUN	JUL
Sales							
Boat sales	$15,000	$10,000	$60,000	$100,000	$100,000	$80,000	$40,000
Accessories and parts sales	5,000	10,000	30,000	30,000	30,000	30,000	25,000
Repairs & accessory installation	20,000	40,000	50,000	60,000	75,000	65,000	50,000
Total sales	40,000	60,000	140,000	190,000	205,000	175,000	115,000
Cost of sales							
Boats	11,250	7,500	45,000	75,000	75,000	60,000	30,000
Parts & accessories	3,000	6,000	18,000	18,000	18,000	18,000	15,000
Direct labor	6,600	13,200	16,500	19,800	26,400	23,100	16,500
Sales commission	2,000	3,000	7,000	9,500	10,250	8,750	5,750
Total cost of sales	22,850	26,700	86,500	122,300	129,650	109,850	67,250
Gross profit	17,150	30,300	53,500	67,700	75,350	65,150	47,750
General & administrative expenses							
Executive & admin. salaries	11,000	11,000	11,000	11,000	11,000	11,000	11,000
Advertising	3,000	3,000	3,000	3,000	3,000	3,000	3,000
Rent	3,000	3,000	3,000	3,000	3,000	3,000	3,000
Utilities	500	500	500	500	500	500	500
General insurance	400	400	400	400	400	400	400
Legal and accounting fees	4,000	500	500	500	500	500	500
Telephone & Internet expense	500	500	500	500	500	500	500
Office supplies	400	100	100	100	100	100	100
Vehicle expenses	600	600	600	600	600	600	600
Travel expenses	2,500						
Licenses and fees							
Depreciation	2,583	2,583	2,583	2,583	2,583	2,583	2,583
Total general & admin. exp.	28,483	22,183	22,183	22,183	22,183	22,183	22,183
Net operating income (loss)	(11,333)	8,117	31,317	45,517	53,167	42,967	25,567
Other expense, interest	1,667	1,645	1,623	1,602	1,579	1,557	1,535
Net income before tax	(13,000)	6,472	29,694	43,915	51,588	41,410	24,032
Federal income tax	(3,939)	1,961	8,997	13,306	15,631	12,547	7,282
Net income after tax	($9,061)	$4,511	$20,697	$30,309	$35,957	$28,863	$16,751

Table 4-2: F & S Monthly Income Statement

FLOATEM & SINKEM BOAT SALES & REPAIR

	AUG	Forecast of Monthly Income Statement SEP	OCT	NOV	DEC	First Year (Part II) YEAR TOTALS
Sales						
Boat sales	$25,000	$20,000	$20,000	$10,000	$30,000	$510,000
Accessories and parts sales	20,000	20,000	20,000	10,000	30,000	265,000
Repairs & accessory installation	40,000	30,000	20,000	20,000	10,000	480,000
Total sales	85,000	75,000	60,000	40,000	70,000	1,255,000
Cost of sales						
Boats	18,750	15,000	15,000	7,500	22,500	382,500
Parts & accessories	12,000	15,000	12,000	6,000	18,000	159,000
Direct labor	13,200	9,900	6,600	6,600	3,300	161,700
Sales commission	4,250	3,750	3,000	2,000	3,500	62,750
Total cost of sales	48,200	43,650	36,600	22,100	47,300	765,950
Gross profit	36,800	31,350	23,400	17,900	22,700	489,050
General & administrative expenses						
Executive & admin. salaries	11,000	11,000	11,000	11,000	11,000	132,000
Advertising	3,000	3,000	3,000	3,000	3,000	36,000
Rent	3,000	3,000	3,000	3,000	3,000	36,000
Utilities	500	500	500	500	500	6,000
General insurance	400	400	400	400	400	4,800
Legal and accounting fees	500	500	500	500	1,000	10,000
Telephone & Internet expense	500	500	500	500	500	6,000
Office supplies	100	100	100	100	100	1,500
Vehicle expenses	600	600	600	600	600	7,200
Travel expenses			2,000			2,000
Licenses and fees					3,000	5,500
Depreciation	2,583	2,584	2,584	2,584	2,584	31,000
Total general & admin. exp.	22,183	22,184	24,184	22,184	25,684	278,000
Net operating income (loss)	14,617	9,166	(784)	(4,284)	(2,984)	211,050
Other expense, interest	1,512	1,489	1,466	1,443	1,420	18,539
Net income before tax	13,105	7,677	(2,250)	(5,727)	(4,404)	192,511
Federal income tax	3,971	2,326	(682)	(1,735)	(1,334)	58,329
Net income after tax	$9,134	$5,351	($1,569)	($3,992)	($3,069)	$134,182

Table 4-2: F & S Monthly Income Statement

FLOATEM & SINKEM BOAT SALES & REPAIR — Forecast of Monthly Cash Flow Statement — First Year (Part I)

	JAN	FEB	MAR	APR	MAY	JUN	JUL
Cash inflows							
Investment by owners	$100,000						
Proceeds of bank loan	200,000						
Cash from sales	27,500	$43,750	$121,250	$180,500	$196,000	$177,750	$126,500
Total cash inflows	327,500	43,750	121,250	180,500	196,000	177,750	126,500
Cash outflows							
Boat purchases	100,000	20,000	40,000	50,000	80,000	80,000	50,000
Equipment purchase	150,000			5,000			
Parts & accessory purchases	50,000	10,000	30,000	30,000	20,000	20,000	15,000
Deposits on rent, utilities, etc.	4,500						
Direct labor	6,600	13,200	16,500	19,800	26,400	23,100	16,500
Sales commissions	2,000	3,000	7,000	9,500	10,250	8,750	5,750
Executive & admin. salaries	11,000	11,000	11,000	11,000	11,000	11,000	11,000
Advertising	3,000	3,000	3,000	3,000	3,000	3,000	3,000
Rent	3,000	3,000	3,000	3,000	3,000	3,000	3,000
Utilities		500	500	500	500	500	500
General insurance	400	400	400	400	400	400	400
Legal and accounting fees	4,000	500	500	500	500	500	500
Telephone & Internet expense		500	500	500	500	500	500
Office supplies		400	100	100	100	100	100
Vehicle expenses		600	600	600	600	600	600
Travel expenses	2,500						
Licenses and fees							
Loan payment, P & I	4,249	4,249	4,249	4,249	4,249	4,249	4,249
Estimated income tax payments				14,582		14,582	
Total outflows	341,249	70,349	117,349	152,732	160,499	170,282	111,099
Net cash flow for period	(13,749)	(26,599)	3,901	27,768	35,501	7,468	15,401
Cash at beginning of period		(13,749)	(40,349)	(36,448)	(8,680)	26,821	34,289
Cash at end of period	($13,749)	($40,349)	($36,448)	($8,680)	$26,821	$34,289	$49,690

Table 4-3: F & S Monthly Cash Flow Statement

FLOATEM & SINKEM BOAT SALES & REPAIR

Forecast of Monthly Cash Flow Statement

	AUG	SEP	OCT	NOV	DEC	First Year (Part II) YEAR TOTALS
Cash inflows						
Investment by owners						$100,000
Proceeds of bank loan						200,000
Cash from sales	$95,500	$79,750	$68,250	$47,250	$66,500	1,230,500
Total cash inflows	95,500	79,750	68,250	47,250	66,500	1,530,500
Cash outflows						
Boat purchases	15,000					435,000
Equipment purchase						155,000
Parts & accessory purchases	10,000	5,000	5,000	10,000	10,000	215,000
Deposits on rent, utilities, etc.						4,500
Direct labor	13,200	9,900	6,600	6,600	3,300	161,700
Sales commissions	4,250	3,750	3,000	2,000	3,500	62,750
Executive & admin. salaries	11,000	11,000	11,000	11,000	11,000	132,000
Advertising	3,000	3,000	3,000	3,000	3,000	36,000
Rent	3,000	3,000	3,000	3,000	3,000	36,000
Utilities	500	500	500	500	500	5,500
General insurance	400	400	400	400	400	4,800
Legal and accounting fees	500	500	500	500	1,000	10,000
Telephone & Internet expense	500	500	500	500	500	5,500
Office supplies	100	100	100	100	100	1,400
Vehicle expenses	600	600	600	600	600	6,600
Travel expenses			2,000			2,000
Licenses and fees					3,000	5,500
Loan payment, P & I	4,249	4,249	4,249	4,249	4,249	50,993
Estimated income tax payments		14,582			14,582	58,329
Total outflows	66,299	57,082	40,449	42,449	58,732	1,388,572
Net cash flow for period	29,201	22,668	27,801	4,801	7,768	141,928
Cash at beginning of period	49,690	78,890	101,558	129,359	134,160	
Cash at end of period	$78,890	$101,558	$129,359	$134,160	$141,928	$141,928

Table 4-3: F & S Monthly Cash Flow Statement

Inventory is an asset, and assets show up on a balance sheet, which is Table 4-4 on page 143. (As is usually the case, the bank did not request monthly balance sheets, so only the year-end balance sheet was created.) The same concept happens for the parts and accessories purchases: only $3,000 as a cost in January; the other $47,000 is an inventory item.

Notice the line for telephone and Internet expense. There is no cash outflow in January, and that's because the bill from the telephone company will not arrive until February. In other words, the company will always pay its telephone bill 30 days after it has used the service, so it always owes the phone company for that one month of service. The same story applies to utilities, office supplies, and vehicle expense. Those always-trailing expenses comprise the accounts payable figure in the balance sheet.

Let's return to the Floatem & Sinkem story.

After looking at the cash flow statement, the banker raised the prospect that the company might go out of business in February, before it really got started, as there would be a negative cash balance of $40,349. Floyd and Sidney discussed the possibility of holding back on boat purchases until the cash flow improved later in the year. However, this would mean that were no boats to sell, so they would miss out on the boat sales that were to be a substantial part of their income. Because that was a poor idea, the consensus of the banker and the entrepreneurs was that the loan request should be increased to $300,000. That meant that some preliminary paperwork already submitted to the Small Business Administration would have to be revised, but that's the sort of hassle that's inherent in dealing with a bureaucracy. Another part of that

Floatem & Sinkem Sales & Repair
Forecast of Balance Statement
End of First Year

Current assets:		
Cash	$ 141,928	
Accounts receivable	24,500	
Inventory parts & accessories	56,000	
Inventory boats	52,500	
Deposits	4,500	
Total current assets		$ 279,428
Fixed assets:		
Equipment	155,000	
Subtract accumulated depreciation	31,000	
		124,000
Total assets		403,428
Liabilities and stockholders' equity:		
Current liabilities		
Accounts payable	1,700	
Loan payable	167,546	
Total liabilities		169,246
Stockholders' equity:		
Common stock	100,000	
Retained earnings	134,182	
Total equity		234,182
Total liabilities & stockholders'equity		$ 403,428

Table 4-4: F & S Balance Sheet

process was a revision of the monthly cash flow statement to reflect the larger cash inflow. It also caused revision of the monthly income statement, because interest expense would be higher and that would cause some reduction in the federal income tax,[4] which then would change the net income.

The Process of Preparing Forecasted Financial Statements

As you can see from the Floatem & Sinkem example, the process of creating forecasted cash flows and other financial statements is one of trial and error. In the paper, pencil, and calculator era, it could take a copious amount of time. Today, with electronic spreadsheets and the capability of creating functions and formulas within them, life as a little easier. Once set up in a spreadsheet program, you can play "what if" until you get it just right.

For an alternative, you can purchase software with the formulas and links ready to go. The downside is that off-the-shelf products inherently have some inflexibility and, therefore, may be difficult to apply to your situation.

By the way, if you look at financial statements of publicly traded companies, you'll find the cash flow statement to be quite dissimilar to what is in this book. The reason is that the readers of these documents have two different needs. The format in this book is for planning and analysis of company history and forecasts by management, wheras the format in published financial statements is for analysis by investors and their advisors. The former has a higher interest in making cash flow happen month-by-month. The latter is interested in what did happen last year and what might happen this year.

Your Business Plan

If you've ever created a business plan or have read a book on how to create one, you probably realize that accomplishing a cash forecast also creates a major part of a business plan. In fact, in creating an internal cash flow forecast (that is, one that is used only by the management of a company), you have already created a business plan. So, if your cash flow forecast indicates that you need to talk to your banker now (not later), all you need to do is add your historical financial statements and polish up your presentation of the underlying facts (sales, costs, overhead, and so forth). Of course, if you're planning a new business and seeking to borrow funds, you can substitute a financial history of the business owners for the historical statements of the business.

These things we have done to create cash flow projections are also the heart of a business plan.

Your Future

In this book, I've tried to offer suggestions on financing your enterprise, conserving the cash that it earns, and planning your cash flow realistically. Above all, I hope I have convinced you that adequate capital (yours or someone else's) is a prerequisite to success in business. So, take the time to plan your cash needs and make sure they are covered. Then, when you're successful, others will admire your "luck," but you and I will know better—it was lots of planning and just plain hard work.

Appendices

Appendix A:

Annual Rate of Return of Cash Discount

When you pay in time to take a cash discount, what is the interest rate that you are earning on your money?

Say a vendor allows you to take a 2-percent discount if you pay by the 10th of the month but allows no cash discount if you pay later. The last day you can pay the invoice without being delinquent is the 30th of the month. In effect, if you pay at the end of the month, you have given up 2 percent of the invoice in exchange for keeping your money for another 20 days.

In every year, there are 18 20-day periods ($360 \div 20 = 18$), so 2 percent every 20 days is the equivalent of $18 \times 2\%$ or 36 percent per year.

> Moral: Take the discount. It's hard to come by 36-percent investments every month.

Appendix B:

Internal Control

In the discussion of methods of handling cash receipts, such as a lockbox, I referred to "internal control." You can find a long-winded definition in accounting textbooks, but in plain language, it's setting up your internal systems so that it is almost impossible for someone to carry your whole store out the back door. By internal systems, I mean not just the backroom bookkeeping systems, but the whole process of running a business—ordering material and services, receiving materials and services, receiving and auditing invoices, writing checks, selling your product and services, receiving the cash for those sales, and guarding the cash with safekeeping in a bank, safe, or mattress.

For an example of the internal control of a "front end" in a merchandise operation, consider a large retail store or "club store" operation. The customer brings a piece of merchandise to a cashier, who scans the bar code (no opportunity to ring up the item at a reduced price for a friend) and collects the money from the customer. The cash register (really a computer terminal) adds the total amount of a cash sale to the cash that should be in the cash drawer, so there is no opportunity for the cashier to siphon off a few dollars into his or her pocket. For a sale charged to a credit card, the cash register keeps track of how much should be the total of signed charge slip in the cash drawer. (A cashier can't throw away a charge slip for a friend without being short.) Of course, the gaping hole in the internal control of this cash register operation is the cashier who "forgets" to scan an item for a friend. That's why there are closed circuit television cameras and video recorders operating at strategic locations in the store—the store security people are watching. Beyond that, some stores post a checker at the exit door who is supposed to make sure that every item in the cart is listed on the sales receipt the cash register generated for the customer.

At the same time the cash register and the main computer is keeping track of cash and credit cards, they are also keeping track of inventory. When merchandise is delivered to the store, it is counted. Then the quantity of merchandise received is entered into the computer, which checks the count against the purchase order and the vendor's shipping document. (Those figures won't match if the receiving crew is siphoning off goods to the cargo area of their SUVs.) The computer also adds the count to the inventory on hand. When the items are sold to customers, the cash register deducts them from inventory. If the computer count of inventory doesn't match the count of the item on the shelves, management knows quickly and can look for the leak (more closed circuit television cameras).

Back to the cash again, the computer adds up the cash received from all of the cash registers and compares that with the daily deposit of cash into the bank. If they don't match, management is again aware very quickly and can take action, as in fire someone or even turn the problem over to the local prosecutor's office.

It's difficult for a small business without sophisticated computerized cash registers, computerized inventory records, closed circuit television, and so on to be able to match the big stores' internal control. An entrepreneur needs constantly to be aware of this and install whatever internal control he or she can. The bank lockbox is one such control. Cash and checks that never come into the store or office can't be diverted by a dishonest employee. The installation of video cameras, even fake ones, can help discourage theft. Security consultants, system designers, and accountants can help you do all that you can to plug a cash outflow that sinks thousands of small businesses every year.

Appendix C:

Collection Letters

The following five letters and procedures should help you write your own collection letters and give you ideas on how to proceed.

First Collection Letter

This first collection letter is designed to appear as a routine form that is generated by a computerized billing system or by an office clerk. Everyone knows that stuff happens: Invoices disappear, merchandise arrives broken, shortages happen, and so on. Don't risk the good will of your customers by insinuating that they are trying to beat you out of a bill this early in the process. For the same reason, avoid signing the letter as "collection department." Suggestions: Financial Department, Bookkeeper, Auditing Department, Problem Resolution Department, or whatever else that is relatively innocuous. See the example on page 156.

[Date]

[Customer's name and address]

Attention: Accounts Payable
          [if it's a business account]

Dear Customer:

Our records indicate that the following invoice(s) remains outstanding in your account:

[List dates, number, and amount of invoice(s).]

Perhaps our original invoice went astray, so if you need another copy, please call us for one, or e-mail us at: [fill in e-mail address].

If, by chance, there is another problem with our invoice, please let us know so that we can correct any error.

Thank you in advance for your prompt response to this letter.

Financial Department

Second Collection Letter

This letter is a little stronger and lets the customer know that the time has passed for saying that the nonpayment is due to oversight or other error. See the example on page 158.

[Date (15 days after the first letter)]

[Customer's name and address]

Attention: Accounts Payable
                      [if it's a business account]

Dear Customer:

Did our invoice and follow-up letter both go astray? We wrote you 15 days ago about the following invoice(s):

[List dates, number, and amount of invoice(s).]

These charges are rapidly aging, so please write us a check or tell us why payment is not forthcoming.

Thank you for your attention to this matter.

Sincerely,

[Some individual should sign this one.]

Credit Department

Third Collection Activity

If there has been no response to the first or second letter by 15 days after the second letter, it is time to make telephone contact. If you do not already know who is in charge of paying bills at your customer's operation, finding out that information should be the first goal of your call. The second goal is to talk to that individual and ask for quick payment. Depending on the results of your phone call, send a letter to the effect of one of the two examples on pages 160 and 161. Modify them to fit the circumstances.

[Date]

[Customer's name and address]

Dear [the individual in charge who you talked to]:

I'm glad we had the opportunity to discuss the invoice of [date] in the amount of $[invoice total].

As you say you do not have a record of receiving the merchandise, I am enclosing a merchandise receipt signed by [name] on [date].

I trust that document will enable you to forward payment to us. However, if there is any other problem, please call me.

Thank you for your help.

Yours truly,

[Personal signature]

[Title]

[Date]

[Customer's name and address]

Dear [the individual in charge, whose name you found out by telephone]:

I regret I was not able to contact you by telephone yesterday. The subject of my call and the message I left is the unpaid invoice of [date] for $[amount].

As you are probably aware, this item is now over 45 days past due, so it deserves immediate attention. Please send us a check, or call, write, or e-mail the reason for nonpayment.

Yours truly,

[Personal signature]

[Title]

Fourth Collection Activity

At this point you should know what sort of collection problem you have. If the cause for nonpayment in the first situation is really a missing piece of paper, but you have not received a check in another 10 or 15 days, a friendly follow-up call may be all that is needed.

In the second case, when the person in charge will not even return your phone call, it is time to get tough, although you can try one other avenue first. That is to call the assistant of the individual in charge or, lacking that, his or her boss. If that fails, it is time to send the letter on page 163.

Once you have threatened legal action, be sure to follow up by actually referring the matter to an attorney.

CERTIFIED MAIL #
  [certified mail receipt number]
RETURN RECEIPT REQUESTED
DELIVER ONLY TO ADDRESSEE

[Individual's name]
[Company]
[Title]
  Re: Our invoice #[invoice number] of [date]
        in the amount of $[invoice total]

Dear [individual's name]:

   In the matter of this unpaid invoice that is now [actual number of] days past due, we have sent you three letters and have made five attempts to reach you by telephone, leaving a message asking for a return call on each of those occasions. Obviously, we are disappointed that you have neither remitted payment nor contacted us as to the reason for nonpayment.

   Please be advised, therefore, that unless payment is in our hands within seven (7) days from the date you receive this letter, we will have no choice but to refer this to our collection attorney for appropriate action.

Yours truly,

[Individual signature]

[Title]

Modified Collection Effort

Of course, there are situations in between the extremes illustrated by the two collection challenges in the fourth collection activity. If your debtors acknowledge that they owe you but are unable to pay due to the persistent disease of "no-money-itis," a patient period of working with them may be your best bet. If you go to court and get a judgment, and the individual or company has no free-and-clear assets, all you have done is run up a lawyer's bill and created another judgment that may hinder the debtor from generating the funds with which to pay you.

Although you may be able to work out a protracted schedule of payments by letter, a phone call or a face-to-face meeting usually works better. Be sure to confirm any arrangement by letter, and include in the letter the fact that the debtor will have to pay cash-on-delivery for future merchandise or services.

Appendix D:

Employee vs. Self-Employed Contractor

This is from the Internal Revenue Service's Publication number 15-A, "Employer's Supplemental Tax Guide." It concerns the rules as to whether someone who is providing personal services to your business is an employee or a contractor. This significantly affects your cash flow, as you usually are not responsible for withholding or payroll tax for a self-employed contractor.

Make this determination of status carefully and with professional advice. If you incorrectly classify an individual as a contractor when he or she is actually an employee, the IRS could wipe you out. You would be liable for the income and social security tax that you should have withheld, as well the taxes levied on you as the employer, plus (the worst part) severe penalties and some interest.

What is reprinted here are the basic rules for determination of the status of an individual insofar as the IRS is concerned. Publication 15-A goes into much detail and discusses certain cases and industries. If the rules here pique your curiosity as to whether you could classify people as contractors rather than employees, call the IRS and order the full Publication 15-A (or download it from the Internet).

If, after reading what's here and the publication you can order, you're in doubt, the IRS will help you. You can file Form SS-8 with the IRS, giving the IRS people an explanation of your situation, and receive a reply as to whether your situation calls for classification as an employee or a contractor. As the expectation may be that the IRS will err toward classification as an employee, you may want to consult a nongovernment tax professional instead.

Here is how the IRS explains the rules:

Employee or Independent Contractor

An employer must generally withhold income taxes, withhold and pay social security and Medicare taxes, and pay unemployment tax on wages paid to an employee. An employer does not generally have to withhold or pay any taxes on payments to independent contractors.

Common-Law Rules

To determine whether an individual is an employee or an independent contractor under the common law, the relationship of the worker and the business must be examined. All evidence of control and independence must be considered. In any employee/independent contractor determination, all information that provides evidence of the degree of control and the degree of independence must be considered.

Facts that provide evidence of the degree of control and independence fall into three categories: behavioral control, financial control, and the type of relationship of the parties. These facts are discussed in the sections that follow.

Behavioral Control

Facts that show whether the business has a right to direct and control how the worker does the task for which the worker is hired include the type and degree of the two following aspect:

Instructions the Business Gives the Worker

An employee is generally subject to the business' instructions about when, where, and how to work. All of the following are examples of types of instructions about how to do work:

✦ When and where to do the work.

✦ What tools or equipment to use.

✦ What workers to hire or to assist with the work.

✦ Where to purchase supplies and services.

✦ What work must be performed by a specified individual.

✦ What order or sequence to follow.

The amount of instruction needed varies among different jobs. Even if no instructions are given, sufficient behavioral control may exist if the employer has the right to control how the work results are achieved. A business may lack the knowledge to instruct some highly specialized professionals; in other cases, the task may require little or no instruction. The key consideration is whether the business has retained the right to control the details of a worker's performance or instead has given up that right.

Training the
Business Gives the Worker

An employee may be trained to perform services in a particular manner. Independent contractors ordinarily use their own methods.

Financial Control

Facts that show whether the business has a right to control the business aspects of the worker's job include:

The Extent to Which the Worker
Has Unreimbursed Business Expenses

Independent contractors are more likely to have unreimbursed expenses than are employees. Fixed ongoing costs that are incurred regardless of whether work is currently being performed are especially important. However, employees may also incur unreimbursed expenses in connection with the services they perform for their business.

The Extent of
the Worker's Investment

An independent contractor often has a significant investment in the facilities he or she uses in performing services for someone else. However, a significant investment is not necessary for independent contractor status.

The Extent to Which
the Worker Makes Services
Available to the Relevant Market

An independent contractor is generally free to seek out business opportunities. Independent contractors often advertise, maintain a visible business location, and are available to work in the relevant market.

How the Business Pays the Worker

An employee is generally guaranteed a regular wage amount by the hour, week, or other period of time. This usually indicates that a worker is an employee, even when the wage or salary is supplemented by a commission. An independent contractor is usually paid by a flat fee for the job. However, it is common in some professions, such as law, to pay independent contractors hourly.

The Extent to Which the Worker Can Realize a Profit or Loss

An independent contractor can make a profit or loss.

Type of Relationship

Facts that show the parties' type of relationship include:

+ Written contracts describing the relationship the parties intended to create.

+ Whether the business provides the worker with employee-type benefits, such as insurance, a pension plan, vacation pay, or sick pay.

+ The permanency of the relationship. If you engage a worker with the expectation that the relationship will continue indefinitely, rather than for a specific project or period, this is generally considered evidence that your intent was to create an employer-employee relationship.

+ The extent to which services performed by the worker is a key aspect of the regular business of the company. If a worker provides services that are a key aspect of your regular business activity, it is more likely that you will have the right to direct and control his or her activities. For example, if a law firm hires an attorney, it is likely that it will present the attorney's work as its own and would have the right to control or direct that work. This would indicate an employer-employee relationship.

Appendix E:

Partial Loan Guarantee Financing by the SBA

Quoted From the SBA Website:

The SBA enables its lending partners to provide financing to small businesses when funding is otherwise unavailable on reasonable terms by guaranteeing major portions of loans made to small businesses.

The Agency does not currently have funding for direct loans nor does it provide grants or low interest rate loans for business start-up or expansion.

The eligibility requirements and credit criteria of the program are very broad in order to accommodate a wide range of financing needs.

When a small business applies to a lending partner for a loan, the lender reviews the application and decides if it merits a loan on its own or if it requires additional support in the form of an SBA guaranty. SBA backing on the loan is then requested by the lender. In guaranteeing the loan, the SBA assures the lender that, in the event the borrower does not repay the loan, the government will reimburse the lending partner for a portion of its loss.

By providing this guaranty, the SBA is able to help tens of thousands of small businesses every year get financing they would not otherwise obtain.

To qualify for an SBA guaranty, a small business must meet the SBA's criteria, and the lender must certify that it could not provide funding on reasonable terms without an SBA guaranty.

The SBA can guarantee as much as 85 percent on loans of up to $150,000 and 75 percent on loans of more than $150,000. In most cases, the maximum guaranty is $1 million. There are higher loan limits for International Trade, defense-dependent small firms affected by defense reductions, and Certified Development Company loans.

For more details, direct your internet browser to the SBA Website at *www.sba.gov/financing/*.

Appendix F:

Creating a Business Plan

I cannot emphasize too strongly that outlines and sample business plans should not be followed blindly—**don't fill in all the elements blindly.**

Do make sure that you have backup facts, figures, and other material for everything in the plan. If you can't come up with support for some part of your plan, omit it or label it as "estimated."

Elements of a Business Plan

Here's a list of the elements of a business plan, from the Small Business Administration Website, *www.sba.gov/starting/indexbusplans.html*. Also, see the list of sites with sample business plans at *www.sba.gov/hotlist/businessplans.html*.

1. Cover sheet.

2. Statement of purpose.

3. Table of contents.

I. The Business.

    A. Description of business.

    B. Marketing.

    C. Competition.

    D. Operating procedures.

    E. Personnel.

    F. Business insurance.

    G. Financial data.

II. Financial Data.

    A. Loan applications.

    B. Capital equipment and supply list.

    C. Balance sheet.

    D. Breakeven analysis.

    E. Pro-forma income projections (profit & loss statements).

        1. Three-year summary.

        2. Detail by month, first year.

        3. Detail by quarters, second and third years.

        4. Assumptions upon which projections were based.

    F. Pro-forma cash flow.

        1. Follow guidelines for letter E.

III. Supporting Documents.

    1. Tax returns of principals for last three years.

    2. Personal financial statement (all banks have these forms).

    3. In the case of a franchised business, a copy of franchise contract and all supporting documents provided by the franchiser.

    4. Copy of proposed lease or purchase agreement for building space.

    5. Copy of licenses and other legal documents.

    6. Copy of resumes of all principals.

    7. Copies of letters of intent from suppliers, etc.

Chapter
Notes

Chapter 1

[1] The terms *invoice* and *statement* can be confusing. They are often used interchangeably, although they have different meanings. Strictly speaking, an invoice is a document that is prepared at the time a sale is made, listing the items, the prices, and the total charge for all items on that invoice. A statement is sent to the customer at the end of the month and lists all of the invoices rendered to the customer during the month. Its purpose is basically twofold: It makes sure the customer has not misplaced an invoice (which could mean it wouldn't get paid) and it reminds the customer that it's time to write a check.

Many businesses that provide continuing services, such as accountants, lawn-maintenance companies, telephone companies, and many others, combine the information of an invoice nature and a statement nature in one document, which gets labeled "Statement," "Invoice," "Bill," or whatever they choose.

To my knowledge, the grammar police have not pursued correctness in this area and, even if they did, they have no enforcement authority. What you call the documents you send your customers is up to you. Just be sure you send them something that says or infers "pay up!"

For clarity, I have used the strict meanings throughout the text.

Chapter 3

[1] Scott Thurm, "Five High-Tech Companies Are Amassing Big Piles of Cash," *Wall Street Journal*, December 27, 2002.

Chapter 4

[1] In referring to financial documents, the words *forecast* and *projection* are often used interchangeably. However, there is a fine line of distinction: A *forecast* is a document that uses all available factors to make an educated guess as to what will occur in the future. A *projection* takes history and projects it into the future. In other words, the weather bureau forecasts the weather. It can't determine that, because it rained yesterday and this morning, it will continue to rain this afternoon and tomorrow. There are many other factors than just projecting history. On the other hand, if you toss a lighted match into a can of gasoline, we can project the results, inasmuch as we do have a history of people who did that, and from that experience, we can project the result if someone does it again. In a financial document there can be elements of both forecast and projection. For instance, if sales have increased 10 percent per year for a period of five years, and other factors are about the same as in previous years, we can *project* another 10-percent gain in sales. However, if there is now a recession or floodwaters have wiped out half of your market, we can *forecast* a decrease in sales.

Yes, this is nit-picking, but, if you are a purist, this is for you.

[2] What confuses this concept is the fact that the Internal Revenue Service allows small businesses to report some income on a "cash basis." In a way, that amounts to computing

taxes on cash flow instead of on real profits. In this book we are concerned with real profits and real cash flow, so please set aside your tax concerns for now.

[3] For the purposes of this example, we are assuming that the Floatem & Sinkem Boat Sales & Repair is organized as a regular, or C, corporation that pays its own taxes. This may not be the best selection of business form for this situation, but to treat this operation as an S corporation or a limited liability company would involve the personal taxes of the entrepreneurs and hopelessly complicate this example.

[4] State income taxes have been ignored in these financial statements because they vary from state to state, and including them in the calculations would create unnecessary complications for this demonstration.

Index

About the Author

From 30 years of experience as a Certified Public Accountant, Robert Cooke has seen it all, from those small businesspeople who were successful from their start to those who never quite made it. Insight into his experiences can help you be among those who make it.

Before practicing as a CPA, Robert was engaged in the management of several small businesses, including residential construction and a retail hardware store, so he has seen small business from the inside as well as the outside. Other successful business books he has written are *The McGraw-Hill 36-Hour Course in Finance for Nonfinancial Managers, How to Start Your Own S Corporation, Doing Business Tax-Free, Small Business Formation Handbook,* and *Personal Finance for Busy People.*

Robert's education includes a bachelor's degree from Colby College and graduate work at Wharton Graduate School, Old Dominion University, and William and Mary Law School.